A Letter to America

10 Reasons to Give President Bush an Extended Vacation

By

Errington Thompson, M.D.

1663 LIBERTY DRIVE, SUITE 200
BLOOMINGTON, INDIANA 47403
(800) 839-8640
WWW.AUTHORHOUSE.COM

This book is a work of non-fiction. Names of people and places have been changed to protect their privacy.

© *2004 Errington Thompson, M.D.*
All Rights Reserved.

No part of this book may be reproduced, stored in a retrieval system, or transmitted by any means without the written permission of the author.

First published by AuthorHouse 09/03/04

ISBN: 1-4184-9529-8 (sc)
ISBN: 1-4184-9528-X (dj)

Library of Congress Control Number: 2004097029

Printed in the United States of America
Bloomington, Indiana

This book is printed on acid-free paper.

Dedication

To my Mother and Father who stressed education and hard work

To my siblings - Melissa, Michele and Frank

To my wife, Karen, for the love and support that I always need

Table of Contents

Dedication v
Author's Note ix
Chapter 1 – How did we end up with Bush 43? 1
Chapter 2 – Compassionate Conservatism means what, exactly? . 13
Chapter 3 – Leaving Every Child Behind 25
Chapter 4 – The Economy, Tax Cuts and Jobs – The Shell game
with your money and your job 37
Chapter 5 – Terrorism – A lot of running around but 47
Chapter 6 – The Axis: Name Calling – "You're evil." 69
Chapter 7 – Iraq – Dorothy, we're not in Kansas any more 93
Chapter 8 – Religion - See no evil, Hear no evil. 103
Chapter 9 – Environment - please pass me a gas mask 113
Chapter 10 – Leadership – There is a Difference between
Wandering and Leading 125

Author's Note

I have talked about writing a book for decades but I was always too busy. After reading Al Franken's book I was truly inspired. Seven months later, I have completed my book, only 10 week behind my self-imposed schedule.

I would like to thank several people for their help with this book. First, I would to thank Al Gore and like minded congressmen who funded the early internet project. The internet and a credit card made it possible for me to access newspaper and news magazine archives from the comfort of my home. If I would have had to go to the library every day that I worked on this book I would have never been able to complete it without quitting my daytime job. Secondly, I would like to thank Mollie Walker for continuously organizing all of my paperwork without losing anything and Catherine Ross for her editing expertise. Next, thanks to my family (Karen, Kelly, Kristen, Mom, Melissa, Michele, Frank and Marquis) for understanding the crazy notion that a trauma surgeon could write a book on politics.

Thanks to my brothers in medicine, Elton, John, Eddie and Harry for always being there for me.

Being a friend for over 30 years, Kurt Eichenwald needs a special thanks for being an inspiration. He has set a standard in "real" journalism that can only be equaled but never surpassed. I hope that I have lived up to his standard.

I would like to thank the faculty and staff of St. Mark's School of Texas in Dallas. St. Mark's has made my life possible (see chapter 3). I was taught how to think critically. This skill was enhanced by 3 surgeons during my training - Roy Clay, Edwin Deitch and Timothy Buchman. Thanks gentleman for a gift that I use everyday.

Finally, a special thanks to my wife, Karen for reading draft after draft, for always giving me her honest opinion and always encouraging me to do better. I hope that I did do better.

Chapter 1 –
How did we end up with Bush 43?

Dear America,

I've become disturbed by recent events. This letter is my attempt to illuminate the policies and actions of the present Bush administration. Iraq, Iran, Afghanistan, unemployment, the environment, education, foreign-policy, tax cuts, and our energy policy all seem to go against the national mainstream. More and more Americans seem to be disinterested or disenfranchised with politics. I thought that maybe if I could explain events so that they are, perhaps, more clearly articulated, America would also be disturbed by current events. Hopefully, Americans would then understand that being involved in politics is the only way that we will get politicians that reflect our hopes, fears and dreams. I am not a political science major, nor am I one of those talking heads on television. I am a taxpayer, a parent, and a trauma surgeon in a mid-sized American city. I read newspapers, scan internet news web sites, and watch the national news. I am just one of many citizens of the United States; but as such, I believe it is our duty to test, question, and evaluate our leaders. This book details what one American has come to think about our current President, George W. Bush.

I was born in Middle America in 1960. America has experienced unprecedented growth and peace during my lifetime; yet in grade school, we had air raid drills and were told we were in a fight to the death with the Soviet Union. My childhood was touched by the assassinations of the Kennedy brothers, of Malcolm X, and Martin Luther King. My understanding of the presidency of George W. Bush is shaped by what I saw in the other Presidents who led our country while I was growing up.

Nixon is the first president whom I can remember. His impeachment hearings started when I was a teenager, and they imprinted the equivocal phrase, "Not to the best of my recollection," on my brain. "Recollection" was not a word that I had used on a regular basis before the hearings, but for almost a year my friends and I had a new phrase to drive our parents crazy: "Not to the best of my recollection." "Did you clean your room?" "Not to the best of my recollection, Mom." "Did you break that vase?" "Not to the best of my recollection, Mom." Mother was not amused.

Ford's presidency seemed to end before it began. *Saturday Night Live*, which started during Ford's presidency, portrayed him almost every weekend, as tripping and falling over anything they could find to put in his way. For reasons that are not clear, we always found this funny. But despite his regularly mocked clumsiness, Ford did steer the American presidency away from the Nixonian abyss of scandal and helped us to trust our Presidents again. I believe he was the right man at the right time. He was honest. He was endearing. And he probably did the right thing for the county by pardoning Nixon, for this certainly helped the county heal.

Carter followed Ford. He came out of nowhere. He campaigned for several years speaking at local women's groups and civic clubs throughout the country. I do not remember much about his campaign except that, like Ford, he was honest. He would tell us "I don't know" instead of changing the subject or equivocating. The country was still in need of honesty. Carter, like all Presidents, had victories and defeats. As President you would like for your defeats to be during the first two years of your presidency and for your triumphs to come in the last two years, so the citizenry will remember you as a winner. Luck was not with Carter. He had some huge, late-term defeats. The worst, of course, was the Iran hostage crisis. He had no good solution; and, as a result, America looked helpless. A group of third-world thugs with no significant military power held a superpower hostage; indeed, they helped to defeat the honest peanut farmer from Georgia. He tried one rescue attempt in the desert, which failed miserably. Prior to the Iran crisis and the crash of helicopters in the Arabian Desert, Carter was faced with a not-unrelated oil crisis. OPEC, a group about which few of us had ever heard before the late 70's, cornered the market on oil overnight. We all recall how oil production slowed and prices soared. And for the first time since World War II, Americans waited in gasoline lines. Carter rightly pointed out that we use too much oil. Trying to lead us to a more conservative use of energy, he turned down the thermostat in the White House to 65° and addressed the nation in a button-up sweater. When it seemed as though the Arabs really were going to change our lives by withholding their oil, Carter and the United States once again looked powerless. And yet, there was enough oil; and we weren't really powerless. The thing we, as a nation, learned from watching all this is that we never wanted to feel or look powerless again.

As we all know, Carter did not get re-elected in 1980; and as Ronald Reagan became our 40th President, the hostages were released. It looked like Reagan's doing, and perhaps it was. What Americans saw and felt when Reagan came to office was a tall, handsome man, who often rode a big palomino horse. He stood tall and spoke clearly. He had a vision of America being the biggest, strongest, and most righteous nation in the world. This is what we needed, what we wanted to hear. He told us that the world really was divided into those who were good and those who were evil, and that we could tell them apart. He wasn't a career diplomat. He was more like a grandfather, talking to his family in the backyard. He joked with the press as no other President had had the courage to do since JFK. As a matter of fact, he was at his best when young "whippersnapper" type reporters tried to go after him. He would smile indulgently, "There you go again, Geraldo…". We sensed he'd put the naysayer in his place, and we liked this (even when the reporter was right). But for us, Reagan restored the majesty of our presidency. Carter had been congenially informal. Reagan, was that, too; on the other hand, he could "walk with kings." Besides appearing to bring our hostages back, he took on what he called "the evil empire" –the Soviet Union. He bulked up our military with huge budgetary increases. The Soviet Union responded, just as the experts predicted. Without any highly theorized plan, just his belief that Americans were better and should do the right thing, Reagan put pressure on Russia in every way he could. He showed his willingness to take military action in a little country that most of us couldn't find on a map — Granada. He confronted communist-supported rebels in El Salvador. Every year he kept increasing our military budget. The USSR tried to match our efforts, but couldn't. Their system and their economy imploded. The Berlin Wall fell. Who would have thought this was possible? Experts were stunned. But Reagan seemed to have known this would be the outcome from the very beginning, and he was heralded for having almost single-handedly dismantled the Soviet Union. In response, most Americans cheered. No more gas lines. No more hostages. No more communist threat. The world was free for democracy. I recall feeling that we Americans were once again not only the greatest nation on earth, but now we were the only real super power; and we were "bad," in the coolest sense of that word. Don't mess with us, Reagan told the world.

When Reagan's two terms were over, George Bush, Sr., did what any vice President who follows an extremely popular President does. He portrayed himself as Reagan's junior partner. Reagan's smiling sidekick. Of course, this act down-played how truly intelligent and accomplished George Herbert Walker Bush is. [I'm going to use shorthand from now on George H. W. Bush, the father, will be followed by "41", for he was the 41st President of the United States. His son, George W. Bush, will be followed by "43", a reference, I understand the Bushes now use themselves]. The list of important jobs on Bush 41's *curriculum vitae* is long. He served bravely as a fighter pilot in World War II. He left his Eastern Establishment roots behind, moved to West Texas and drilled for oil. He didn't find just a few cups; he found tons of oil. He became a millionaire in his own right. He served in Congress. He was the US's United Nations ambassador for two years. He was appointed the director of the CIA and served well. Finally, he was elected Vice President during one of the most significant times in our nation since World War II. This was a man, perhaps more than any other in recent history, who was clearly qualified to be President. But somehow, this talented man failed to convince us that he had a clear vision for America's future beyond what Ronald Reagan had already given us. Bush was no Reagan; he lacked the charisma. He made affairs of state look complicated again. Rather than looking like the leader of the free world, he was a good crisis manager. His first major crisis—the Iraqi invasion of Kuwait— clearly showed his tremendous organizational skills. His masterstroke was including Arab nations in the action, so that our counter-invasion did not look like America was trying to steal Arab oil, or like Christians were attacking Muslims. Rather, we were helping our Arab allies protect themselves from rogues such as Saddam Hussein. But Bush 41's mildness, his diplomacy, learned over many years of public service, turned out to be a weakness. We "won," but he did not destroy Saddam. As we all know, this set us up for the second American conflict in the Arabian desert—one that gave his son, George W. Bush 43, the man whose presidency I want us all to look at much more carefully in the light of this short presidential history lesson, a platform from which he might prove himself worthy of the presidency that many believe he did not rightfully win.

Despite his seeming victory in Kuwait, George Bush 41 lost his reelection. It was a surprise to many—how could he lose? Perhaps his odd little incident in an American grocery store, where he marveled at laser scanners, tells the story. He was out of touch with every day Americans, and he didn't realize that he couldn't just ride on the laurels of his success with Desert Storm. He needed a vision. He needed Reagan-like panache. Instead, Jay Leno and *Saturday Night Live* once again had a field day with the gaffes of an American President. I laughed along with everyone else at these monologues and skits; but deep down inside, I knew that our presidency was in trouble again. Moreover, we had slipped into a deep recession; and an increase in taxes, passed by a Republican President who had told us, "Read my lips: no new taxes," had not helped matters. There was plenty more, but the bottom line was that once again the American people simply weren't happy with the man in the Oval Office.

William Jefferson Clinton was a lot of things that George Bush 41 was not. Clinton was a Washington outsider, coming from an underprivileged background, yet educated in elite universities; he connected with the lower and middle classes. He was a great favorite of the black community, and he was a proponent of a new kind of middle-of-the-road Democratic liberalism. He expected to take D.C. by storm. He had hundreds of ideas; many of them good ones. And he beat an incumbent President based upon his "it's the economy, stupid" campaign and a whole lot of personal charm. But this young President's first major initiative was gays in the military. *Gays in the military?* No one would argue that the military establishment has narrow, unfair, and reactionary attitudes about alternative lifestyles; but such a gamble, when the gay and lesbian community wasn't even pushing it themselves, was naïve at best. It became immediately clear that the military would fight a man they labeled "a draft dodger," and it didn't help matters that the rest of America was lukewarm on this issue as well.

Clinton's political judgment was further damaged in the public's eye by his efforts at health-care reform. First, he placed his wife Hillary Rodham Clinton, a non-elected official, in charge of this huge program. Her methods were heavy-handed, and there was no reason for the secrecy that was employed as she developed her plan. Moreover, she almost completely excluded medical groups from the development and planning of this huge project. Like the generals before them, doctors, hospital administrators, and the insurance industry began to protest even before any particulars of the proposed program were announced. The way the whole issue was handled set back meaningful health care reform for decades, and it played into the hands of a suspicious, heavily Republican Congress.

A Letter to America

The Republicans attacked Democrats for being out of touch with mainstream America. Newt Gingrich was able to orchestrate the Republican revolution; a movement that would help pave the way for the election of George W. Bush 43.

Fortunately, Clinton was a fairly quick learner, and he recovered from these early gaffes. He discovered ways to use the budgetary process to infuse funds to programs that he loved such as Head Start (which grew by $3.5 billion during his presidency), Earned Income Tax Credit (which was expanded by over $17 billion), and AmeriCorps (which grew by $100 million); and these moves improved his image with much of his base. A Rhodes Scholar, who is said to read a book every night with almost perfect recall, Clinton boned up on foreign-policy. He did more to try to solve the complex and confusing problems of the Israeli-Palestinian problem than any other President since Jimmy Carter, bringing together leaders from both sides for long and sometimes fruitful negotiations in Washington. In addition to this, Clinton's administration, under the wise eye first of Lloyd Bentsen then of Robert Rubin, as Secretaries of the Treasury, as well as other scholarly economic advisors, worked to improve the economy, as Clinton had promised in his campaign. He was responsible, in some part, for the boom in the computer and the dot-com, industries.

On the other hand, for Clinton, several troublesome lawsuits plagued him throughout his presidency. The Whitewater trading scandal seemed to start a frenzy of attacks on the President. This group unearthed Clinton's "bimbo problem," and America became aware that their President's private sexual appetites, which were certainly hinted at in the campaign when Gennifer Flowers surfaced, was not solved. When the pathetic Monica Lewinsky affair came to light, and Special Prosecutor Kenneth Starr began scrabbling around in the President's private life and his wife's business affairs, it became almost impossible for Clinton to get anything done in his last eighteen months in office. America was once again embarrassed by its President's unethical behavior. Republicans capitalized on the tawdriness of the Monica affair, and reminded the country of the genteel, upright President they had pushed out of office for this over-sexed upstart. The Monica affair, leading to Clinton's impeachment hearings and the degrading image of the President of the United States quibbling on national television with a young lawyer from the Special Prosecutor's office over the meaning of the word "is," made it possible for the son of the President whom Clinton had ousted eight years before to be elected President in 2000.

The son of a President, George W. Bush 43, had been elected Governor of Texas about the same time as the beginning of the so-called Republican Revolution took hold in national politics. While that movement gained momentum in Washington, George W. Bush 43 ran a straightforward campaign to unseat a popular female Governor, Ann Richards. The younger Bush's strategy was simple: Smile, promise a better tomorrow, and stay away from any specifics. He preached family values. He courted the religious right and won their support. Richards ran a terrible campaign. First she didn't take this challenger seriously, then—too late—she tried to attack him for his inexperience and to laugh at him for being born with a "silver foot in his mouth." Bush 43 smiled and stayed on course, right into the Governor's Mansion. Once in office in Austin, George Bush 43 performed well. He reformed education. He built coalitions across party and partisan group lines. He was so successful, that powerful Republicans and their constituencies recognized his potential as a candidate, and eventually moved him into position to win the Republican Party's nomination to be its presidential candidate in 2000.

In order for Bush 43 to win the Presidency in 2000, several things would have to happen. Al Gore would have to run a terrible campaign. He did that. Bush 43 would have to make sure that his past was never an issue. Bush 43 stayed on message and never deviated. My guess is that after the embarrassment of Clinton, and with our memories of Nixon's shame and Carter's ineptitude, George Bush 43 not only seemed like a chance to go back in time to re-elect his father in 1992, but also the chance to have another Reagan-style leader. George Bush 43 projected the image of a God-fearing, straight-talking Christian, a man who had clear and simple ideas about right and wrong, a man without personal ambition, who would do his best for America. We never asked too many questions about his past. The fact that his career before becoming Governor of Texas had not been particularly stellar was never an issue. The fact that he was arrested for drunk driving with a minor in his car in 1976 was never an issue. The fact that he didn't seem to be particularly well-informed about matters of foreign affairs was also not much of an issue for the everyday American. In the debates he was warm, and funny, and he didn't sweat like Al Gore. After beating John McCain in South Carolina, Bush 43 began to look more "Presidential." He said the right things about the economy, the environment, and defense. Al Gore never seemed to connect to core Democrats. He developed no die-hard campaigners who would go the extra mile for him as 43 did. Bush 43 connected with the Far Right and the Young Republicans. As a result, George W. Bush was elected at the 43rd President of the United States.

Chapter 2 – Compassionate Conservatism means what, exactly?

We have all heard the term *compassionate conservatism*. The term was used hundreds of times in the 2000 presidential election. It was in the paper, on the television, and on the radio. George W. Bush "43" is *the* compassionate conservative.

We are all thoughtful individuals, but I'm not sure we all understand the term *compassionate conservatism*. What does it mean? Let's dissect the term. According to *Merriam-Webster's Collegiate Dictionary, compassion* means the sympathetic consciousness of others' distress together with a desire to alleviate it. *Compassionate* is defined as having or showing compassion; the listed synonym is *sympathetic*. Therefore, a compassionate person should be someone with feeling and empathy for others. Well, this is great. As an

American citizen, I want a President who understands and feels my pain. One who relates to *me*. Every American would want this.

Unfortunately, this is an impossible task. Who could possibly empathize with everyone in a country of over 280 million people? And even if our numbers weren't so huge, America is the true melting pot. We have over 140 different Native American tribes alone, each with its own distinct language, history, and customs. What about all of the immigrant groups in our nation? With their languages and history and customs? Even within one tribe or ethnic group, the members will have different opinions, thoughts, and issues. Some of us are employed. Some are homeless. Some live in gated, crimeless neighborhoods. Some live in the ghetto. Some are Catholics, or Methodists, or Hassidic Jews. Some like classical music; others go for country or rap. Some volunteer to serve their country. Others protest against the conflicts and wars in which these volunteers end up serving. Obviously, it is impossible to empathize with everyone. The goal of the President should be to have compassion for most of us.

OK, back to Merriam-Webster, *conservatism* is defined as the principles and policies of the conservative party; the disposition in politics to preserve what is established; a political philosophy based on tradition and social stability, stressing established institutions and preferring gradual development to abrupt change. This doesn't seem so bad. What could be bad about gradual change? Preserving tradition and social stability is a good idea. Therefore, a good, compassionate *conservative* would have empathy for you and me *and* would endeavor to create gradual change and to safeguard social stability.

Is George W. Bush 43 a compassionate conservative? This is the big question. Let us investigate the data. We clearly saw the compassion of our President on September 14, 2001. Bush flew to New York after the attacks on the World Trade Center. He met with Governor Pataki and Mayor Giuliani. He wasn't scheduled to speak, but he visited the site. There, he saw an elderly firefighter standing on a fire truck that had been pulled from the rubble. The President stepped up on top of the fire truck alongside the fireman, who offered to step down and give his President a platform to address the gathering crowd. Bush asked the firefighter to stay with him, to stay by his side. We all remember the chanting, "USA, USA." We all remember the President speaking through that tin can of a bullhorn. Someone shouted from the crowd, "We can't hear you." The President responded, "*I* can hear *you*. The rest of the world will hear you. And the people who knocked these buildings down will hear us all soon" (*New York Times*, September 15, 2001). This truly was the perfect response at the perfect time. It was great. I was proud of our President. About thirty minutes later the President met with some of the families of the World Trade Center victims. He took his time and met with every family member present in the Convention Center that day. For over two hours, Mr. Bush laughed, and he cried with them. That was compassionate. We all felt the President's compassion was honest and powerful that day.

In time, to prevent future catastrophes such as 9/11, the President created the Department of Homeland Security (DHS). Evidence after the disaster suggested that poor communication between the many branches of our government responsible for security and intelligence was one reason we were surprised by the attacks on the World Trade Center. According to the Brookings Institute, creating the DHS was the largest reorganization of the government in over fifty years. By combining several existing agencies into one more efficient department, the President hoped to improve the quality and the flow of information about terrorist groups, so we could protect ourselves better in the future. Correcting the communication flaw is a good idea, an idea that is, at bottom, compassionate. But ironically, the President's response was *not* a conservative one, for everyone knows that big government is a typically liberal Democratic response to crisis.

There is another problem with the creation of the Department of Homeland Security. Security in our land is already the responsibility of many huge arms of the government— the Coast Guard, Immigration, the Secret Service, the FBI, the CIA, and many others. The CIA? The FBI? But these departments were not included in the reorganization plan the President presented. I am a little confused about how you can create a Department of Homeland Security and not include the two largest agencies responsible for security here and abroad. I suppose we must, nevertheless, count the creation of the Department of Homeland Security as a compassionate act, even if it may not be as efficient and information-rich as the press releases about the DHS suggest. But it certainly is not a conservative move, for since time immemorial, Republicans have fought big government tooth and nail.

Besides The Dept. of Homeland Security, our government has an initiative called the Low Income Home Energy Assistance Program, which helps low income families stay warm during the cold winters. This is not an expensive federal project, but it is a compassionate one. According to the National Oceanic and Atmospheric Administration, 2003 was cooler and wetter than normal in the Northeast; this increased the need for expenditures on home heating in that area of the country. But in 2003 President Bush refused to release the $300 million to help these families. Now, this $300 million was earmarked for home energy; it cannot be used for anything else. According to a White House press release on January 24, 2003, President Bush stated, "These funds will help keep our fellow citizens warm in a time of great need and bitter cold. This program is an important source of support for millions of low-income families across the nation." He never gave any explanation for why he would not release the funds earlier. It took a grassroots campaign to get Bush to release these funds. The campaign organized by ACORN, the Association of Community Organizations for Reform Now, a group that works with low and middle income Americans, first moved low-income families into the Republican headquarters in Chicago just prior to a major speech by the President. Then it pressured members of the Senate, which responded with a 88-4 vote to release funds for

LIHEAP; eventually, Bush capitulated. Compassion *under pressure* doesn't ring true.

Where else might we look to assess the compassionate conservativism of George W. Bush? How about unemployment? This is clearly an area that calls for compassion. Over the last four years our economy has sputtered. The jobless rate was 5.6 percent in March of 2004 according to the Bureau of Labor Statistics. The Economic Policy Institute (EPI), a nonprofit, nonpartisan think tank, translates that number into 2.3 million Americans without jobs. This number does not count the number of young adults entering the job market who are unable to find work. Our population is growing. The number of people of working age is also enlarging. Therefore, the economy needed to produce an additional 4.8 million jobs between March 2001 and March 2004. The EPI estimates that it needed to make 7.1 million jobs in order to hold unemployment at 2001 levels. Surely a compassionate President would recognize the need for action in this area. Extending unemployment benefits (states will usually supply twenty-six weeks of unemployment insurance, then the federal government steps in to provide extra coverage) would be one way to show this compassion. But President Bush did not do anything significant about unemployment in 2001, 2002 or most of 2003. Finally in December of 2003 he discussed helping our fellow Americans in his weekly radio address. I just do not understand how a compassionate President could have overlooked so many unemployed citizens for so long. Moreover, when he finally did extend unemployment benefits, a third of those unemployed workers no longer qualified because they had been out of work too long. Maybe Bush thought that his tax cuts would work immediately. Maybe he was trying to be fiscally responsible. One thing is clear; President Bush did not address the issue of unemployment benefits in any major address in over three years. Where's the compassion?

Related to the unemployment problem, our country has been experiencing are the corporate scandals that tore through our economy in 2002. Enron, WorldCom, Tyco. Tens of thousands of workers lost their jobs because incredibly well paid executives were jury-rigging their books. Retirement accounts went from tens of thousands of dollars to zero overnight. Stock losses hurt many Americans as well, when the stock market fluctuated in response to the troubles with industry giants such as Enron and WorldCom. But our compassionate President remained quiet on this subject for months.

The security and exchange commission (SEC) is too under-manned and too underfunded to tackle all the problems uncovered in 2002. The budget for the SEC was $423 million for fiscal year 2001. The Bush administration increased this budget by only 3.5% for fiscal year 2002, which caused the SEC to lay off over fifty employees. Although this seems to be a *conservative* increase in the budget, there does not seem to be any empathy for the workers who have lost their jobs.

Harvey Pitt, chairman of the SEC, a Bush appointee, seemed to be more enamored with big business than with regulating it. The final straw, in his short but tumultuous chairmanship at the SEC, was

Mr. Pitt's hiring of William Webster. Mr. Webster was appointed to head a Congress-mandated inquiry into the accounting scandals. It turned out that Mr. Webster chaired an audit committee of a company that was itself embroiled in scandal. Anyone can make a mistake in appointing the wrong person to the wrong position. Unfortunately, our President never owned up to this mistake. He never stepped forward. He never adequately responded to the thousand of jobs that were lost to corporate malfeasance with any governmental assistance. This seems to be neither compassionate nor conservative.

To move to an entirely different arena where the President might demonstrate his compassion, consider stem cell research. Stem cell research is one of the most promising areas in academic medicine today, it promises to lead to treatments and perhaps even cures or total prevention of serious health problems such as diabetes (which affects over eighteen million Americans per year), Alzheimer's disease (which affects over four million Americans per year), Parkinson's disease (which affects over one million Americans per year) and spinal cord injuries (which affects over ten thousand Americans per year). One problem with stem cell research is that these cells can't be found just anywhere. They are only found in young human embryos. A second problem—a rightly serious one in many people's eyes— is that scientists have to destroy the embryo in order to do this research. It should be understood that the stem cell research debate is different from the abortion debate. Human embryos are the by-products of in vitro fertilization, which is one of the many medical procedures developed out of compassion for childless couples to remedy infertility. The process of in vitro fertilization is inexact at this time, and often that procedure produces far more human embryos than could possibly be used by the families involved in their creation. At present, these extra embryos are either frozen or discarded. If these embryos are going to be thrown away, why can't we use them for good? Why can't we use them for research that could possibly cure someone? It seems that a truly compassionate and conservative President could support this type of initiative. Especially, since this research has the potential to help millions of Americans.

President Bush spent months agonizing over the difficult decision of whether or not to throw governmental support and funding behind stem cell research. Bush stated in his address to the nation, "As a result of private research, more than 60 genetically diverse stem cell lines already exist. They were created from embryos that have already been destroyed, and they have the ability to regenerate themselves indefinitely, creating ongoing opportunities for research. I have concluded that we should allow federal funds to be used for research on these existing stem cell lines, where the life and death decision has already been made." So, President Bush decided that only existing stem cell lines could be used for government-funded research. Moreover, since the government funds over 75% of scientific research in this country, all other stem cell research was effectively halted. Another way to consider how this issue demonstrates our President's compassionate conservativism is this: monies have already been appropriated for this research at the National Institutes of Health. To support the research would not cause any more expenditures of federal funds—*and* such research could possibly cure diseases that cause untold misery.

What is truly remarkable about President Bush's decision about stem cell research is the moral spin that he placed on it. He stated in his August 9, 2001, nationally televised speech that, "Embryonic stem cell research is at the leading edge of a series of moral hazards." There are no moral hazards if we use the tissues created in infertility clinics. You are not stealing eggs from women. You are not removing embryos from the uteri of women against their will. There are no moral hazards. You are using embryos that would otherwise be discarded.

Another argument that President Bush used to justify his decision is "more than sixty genetically diverse stem cell lines already exist." This sounds as though there are plenty of cells for research. This sounds a though a team of scientists can do research on the existing cell lines for years to come. Unfortunately, it is unclear where the number sixty actually came from. To make a long and confusing story short, in a recent CNN.com article, Harvard scientist Dr. Douglas A. Melton stated that there are fifteen cell lines that are available for research. Well, fifteen doesn't sound like much. Fifteen is a whole lot less than sixty. How could the President, who studied this issue for months, who had advice from leading scientists, get his numbers so confused?

Scott Rosenberg of *Salon.com* summed up the stem cell debate best, "Embryos are being destroyed, and will continue to be destroyed, as long as in vitro fertilization is available. Bush's decision doesn't change that. So the only real question is, will these embryos have any meaning or offer anything toward the greater good of humanity? Can anything of value be rescued from their destruction? Can their loss help save other lives?" President Bush does not appear to be compassionate on this subject. Let us look for something else to show is compassionate conservatism.

President Bush has taken on the Taliban in Afghanistan. He has stated that bringing food and medicine to the population of Afghanistan was very important to him. So we should be able to look at our policy toward the "enemy combatants" that are held in Guantánamo Bay, Cuba, and find some compassion. We have been fighting a war against the "evil" Taliban régime for a number of years. Hundreds of Taliban POWs were removed from Afghanistan and flown to Cuba. As prisoners of war, they are entitled to proper treatment, according to the Geneva Convention, which requires that they be released once hostilities are over or tried for crimes against humanity. As POWs or criminals, these people have the right, according to American law, to due process. Some of these prisoners have now been in Cuba for over two years and have not yet seen a lawyer, much less the inside of a court room. Nor have many of them been charged with a specific crime. In his inaugural address President Bush spoke of "America's faith in freedom and democracy." Which part of freedom and democracy are we showing the human beings we are detaining at Guantánamo Bay? If they are guilty, we should try them. Even if they are terrorists, a compassionate leader would give them a fair trial. If they're found guilty, then we would be within our rights, and doing a compassionate thing to exact just punishment. But keeping these people in purgatory for an indefinite length of time is hardly compassionate. Our President has the ability to fix these inhuman conditions, but to date he has not. In this matter, he may be seen as a conservative—being very cautious to protect Americans against possible terrorists. But how compassionate, how moral, or even how legal, is their present treatment, Mr. Bush?

Chapter 3 –
Leaving Every Child Behind

It is hard for me to imagine, writing to you as a trauma surgeon, anything more important than education. This is a subject that I take very seriously. For without education, I clearly could not be a physician. I could not be who I am.

As a third-grader in the Dallas public school system, I was doing extremely well, making straight A's. However, as President of the Parent Teacher Association, my mother noticed several things about my educational experience that troubled her. First, I rarely brought home any homework. Second, I was rewarded for being polite and quiet. For example, I might earn a B on a test for what I had learned, but because I was not a troublemaker, my grade was raised to an A. Finally, my mother observed that the work never seemed to challenge me. After some of what I am sure were extensive and heated discussions between my parents, they enrolled me in a well-respected, private college preparatory school. My life has never been the same since.

This is not a fairy tale. Private school was difficult and at times frustrating. The cultural differences were enormous. But during my ten years at this school, I noticed several constant factors. The teachers expected excellence. They wanted us to learn not just be still and quiet. Every teacher also expected –and almost always got—support from the boys' families, not mindless agreement, but support for their efforts to challenge and stretch our minds. Thanks to a combination of my own personal desire and willingness to adapt, terrific parents, and these supportive, knowledgeable teachers, I soon excelled in this new and challenging environment.

So what can we learn from my experience that can be applied to American public education? There needs to be a three-pronged approach to education. The student, the parents and the teachers must be motivated and willing to do their part. This requires a small, intimate atmosphere where teachers know their students. This approach cannot occur in inner-city schools. The classes are too large. The teachers are too overwhelmed. And the parents are usually too uninvolved.

Several years ago I was watching *Sixty Minutes*. Mike Wallace did a story on David Leven and Michael Feinberg, two thirty year olds who took troubled, inner-city children between the fifth and the eighth grades and turned them into academic powerhouses. The program Leven and Feinberg started is called Knowledge Is Power Program (KIPP). Although the program has been written up in many newspapers and magazine articles, I think most authors miss the extraordinary premise of this educational program — parents, students, and teachers are the primary elements of education—not fancy equipment, computers, or even libraries. Finally, the author of an article in *Forbes Magazine* about KIPP *got it:* the students were expected, just as I was at my prep school, to work hard; and the KIPP designers understood this meant students must devote more time to their education. The Forbes author noted the long hours that are required by the program. The students attend class from eight o'clock in the morning until five o'clock in the afternoon, Monday through Thursday. On Friday the children get out of school at 3:30 P.M. Children are required to attend classes for a half day on Saturday. The children are also expected to attend an extra month of school during the summer. *US News and World Report* noted in 2004 that the KIPP program made it possible for students who were massively underachieving to move ahead of their classmates in very short order. *US News* stressed the "Boot Camp" atmosphere as one of the reasons for the program's success. The article noted that one KIPP school, the South Bronx School, is "a cross between a motivational workshop and a military corps." Slogans like "Work Hard!" "Be Nice!" "There Are No Shortcuts!!" were plastered everywhere. All of these innovations are fine and in some way contribute to the KIPP children's success. But the reason for KIPP's success is simpler than slogans or long hours or rigorous discipline. It is this: When each child starts the program, the child, the parents, and the teachers enter into a formal contract that *everyone* will do his or her best. The child promises to work hard and take his/her studies seriously. The parents are required to promise—*formally*— to do their best to support their children in their academic endeavors. Because a good percentage of these inner city children live in single-parent households, this promise exacts a higher price from these parents than it does from two-parent families—but the single parents of KIPP have responded well to their part of the contract. Finally, the teachers pledge to teach, not just baby-sit. The educators are expected to give their cell phone numbers to their students, so if the students have questions about the homework they can call their teachers at home. The teachers are always available for the children. It is this three-pronged approach that I believe is critical to making American public education more effective. I KNOW it was critical to my success in my early education, and I believe it is critical to the success of KIPP.

The importance of an idea like KIPP on the national educational landscape cannot be underestimated. Anybody can succeed in teaching smart, well-behaved kids who have interested and involved parents. These children have the right environment at home and the right motivation. For the most part, their parents are excellent role models. We all know that large school districts, especially those in our inner cities have complained for decades that their job is too difficult. The students are unmotivated; they are disciplinary problems; they skip school. Their families move from place to place too often, so any kind of continuity in their children's course work becomes impossible. It *would* seem from these complaints that it is simply too hard to do a good job in these public schools. The KIPP program proves that these excuses were simply that – excuses.

In 1998 the results from the Third International Mathematics and Science Study, conducted by International Association for the Evaluation of Educational Achievement, were released. Twenty-one countries took part in the study. This exam covered general math principles and problems as well as general science, such as earth science, life science, physics and chemistry. The Netherlands and Sweden took the honors of first and second, respectively, in mathematics. The United States finished 19th. In science we finished 16th, behind such countries as Taiwan, Singapore, Japan, the Netherlands, England, Belgium, the Russian Federation, the Czech Republic, Slovenia, and Canada. At the time, Richard Riley, the Secretary of Education, remarked that these results were "entirely unacceptable." But these abysmal results should not have been a surprise. Instead, they should be seen as the result of a pattern of increasing educational mediocrity dating from the 1970s. The National Assessment of Educational Progress, conducted by the National Center for Educational Statistics in the US Department of Education, has clearly documented this downward trend in our educational systems.

Every US President since the 70' has confidently stepped up to the plate to improve our public education system. Nixon, Ford, Carter, Reagan, Bush 41, and Clinton have all been in the batter's box and taken their swings. None have made any substantial improvement in the problem. So now we have President George W. Bush. It is his time at the plate. Fortunately, he has tackled this problem before as Governor of Texas. He has a history of improving education.

The education problem in Texas was monumental. Throughout the Sixties and Seventies Texas routinely ranked 49th in education, ahead of only one state—Mississippi. Governor Bush fought for educational reform on many fronts. First, he lent his considerable clout to a 1984 law designed to end social promotion, a law that had not been well enforced. In 1999 Bush pushed a law through the legislature that requires every child in the state to pass the Texas Assessment of Academic Skills Test (TAAS). While well-intentioned, the implementation of this law has been a problem. On the surface, the TAAS program seems like an excellent idea: every child in the state of Texas will be taught the necessary skills and information to pass a demanding test of their basic reading, reasoning, and mathematics skills. Additionally, the law made passing this test a high-stakes enterprise for both school systems and students: schools were punished if their students did not do well on the tests. After three years of a school's poor performance, students at that school would be given a $1500 school voucher that could be used to finance their going to any other school they felt would teach them more effectively. Failing students would be required to repeat the grades in which they failed TAAS tests. So, students were also punished for not performing well on their tests. Whenever the stakes are high, it is human nature to try to cut corners to gain an advantage; educators and students in the State of Texas are no different. Many schools began teaching to the test; students spent an entire school year prepping for TAAS, and many other educational experiences or programs were eliminated. Sadly, there have been reports of students' cheating on the tests as well. After a few years, student test scores on the TAAS did improve, suggesting that our students are learning and retaining more. But during the same time our students' scores on the college entrance exams—the SAT and the ACT—did not change at all. Moreover, an increasing dropout rate in the cities of Houston, Dallas, and San Antonio probably skewed the test results; for if these students had stayed in school and taken their TAAS tests, their scores, most likely, would have lowered those cities' and the state's overall test score average. It would seem that in the case of this particular educational reform, which appeared to be dramatically effective, Governor Bush's efforts made no significant, measurable improvement. He may, in fact, have hurt what was still good in Texas' schools. To continue our baseball analogy, Governor Bush whiffed on a fastball down the middle.

Once Governor Bush became President Bush, he promised that the educational reforms he had instituted in Texas would be implemented nationwide. This policy became known as "No Child Left Behind" (NCLB). This education initiative, which was passed by both houses of Congress, has several important points. First, No Child Left Behind calls for increased accountability on the part of schools for their students' performance. Sanctions such as money being taken from the school's budget and placed into the parents' hands are to be imposed upon schools with high failure rates. Secondly, parents will have the ability, using federal and state dollars, to remove their children from schools with persistently poor test results and to transfer them to better public schools or charter schools.

Several aspects of No Child Left Behind do not seem to make sense. First, is its inflexibility: NCLB doesn't recognize the personal and individualized nature of learning. Ethnic background, family circumstances, a child's own motivation, and teamwork between school and family all affect a child's progress as a learner. But under NCLB schools are rated and sanctioned based upon the average performance of their entire student body. What happens to schools that have high numbers of minority students, or students who are immigrants? In Chicago, for example, 40% of the students in a public school called Waters speak English as their *second* language. How can anyone reasonably expect a school with this kind of teaching burden to score as well as a public school from an affluent neighborhood in which all the children and their parents are native speakers? High failure rates are a serious problem in any state or city that has a large immigrant population. According to a *Time* article, in California, for example, 45% of the schools did not make the NCLB grade last year. In Chicago, another ethnically diverse area, thousands of students did not make the grade.

Another problem with No Child Left Behind is the simple fact that there are not enough places in the better-performing schools for would-be transfer students. For example, in Chicago last year, there were only 1000 spots in the "better" schools into which students (15,000 asked) might transfer. The fact is, at least for the time being, there are not a lot of passing schools with a large number of empty chairs waiting for students to fill them.

So the list of failing schools—what I call "the humiliation list"—is unimaginably long. This is a list, however, that the Bush administration hoped would cause a public outcry and act as a stimulus for local school systems around the country to work harder to reform. But if most schools are on the list, where is the shame? If the mandate of NCLB is simply unattainable for most schools, why would they even try to reform? It seems that President Bush has taken another big swing at the education ball and has come up empty.

Much of the public debate or outcry about No Child Left Behind has focused on the expense and inflexibility of it for administrators (not, surprisingly, on its impact on the nation's children). NCLB has a lot of hidden costs which the states must absorb. Extra testing and system-tracking cost millions of dollars. Where is the money going to come from? Many states are already facing budget shortfalls as it is. Moreover, federal funding appears to be about $15 million short of what is needed to properly implement NCLB. One legislator, James Dillard of Virginia, who is a former teacher, has led an effort to change the law. Dillard has met with Department of Education officials on a number of occasions in order to try to broker some kind of flexibility in the NCLB package. He even met with White House officials, but Dillard reports they simply stonewalled him. In response, Dillard supported a resolution in the Virginia state legislature asking Congress to let Virginia be exempt from NCLB.

In the resolution NCLB was called "the most sweeping intrusion into state and local control of education in the history of the United States." Unfortunately for the Bush administration, Representative Dillard and Virginia are not the only voices calling for major changes in NCLB. Twenty states have jumped on the anti-NCLB bandwagon. Utah has passed a bill that has made it illegal to spend state money on NCLB.

As I have already made clear, at the core of the NCLB fiasco is testing. No where in President Bush's speeches, however, has he made a convincing argument that testing equals learning. Scanning the White House web pages on education, I was unable to find an argument that even touched on this subject. NCLB simply assumes that testing equals knowledge; it presents no evidence in support of this assumption. If, as is now the case, scholars can not agree on whether or not the prestigious SAT, which has a seventy year history, is an effective measure of students' learning, then state tests, which are just now being developed and refined, are certainly in trouble. According to a March 4, 2001, article in *Time Magazine,* "it's getting hard to find an admissions officer anywhere who says an SAT score alone tells you anything important."

There is another controversy about standardized tests, the SAT included: whites and minorities test differently. Many argue that this difference is because most whites in this country are economically advantaged, and therefore either live in better school districts or can buy better education for their children. But even when economic status differences are removed, there is still a gap between the test scores of whites and minorities. Stanford psychologist Claude Steele (*Time* March 4, 2001) took a group of high achieving mixed race students and gave them two tests. He described one test as a problem-solving exercise and the other test as a measure of intelligence. The black children did significantly worse on the intelligence test. The results suggest that blacks perform below their potential when they are told that the test measures intelligence. In essence, they freeze up.

So what does a child sitting in a cold room at 9 o'clock in the morning filling in the answer bubbles on a standardized test with his/her number two pencil really prove to us about education? I'm not sure, but it doesn't seem like our national education policy should be based on testing and testing alone. NCLB has removed a great deal of responsibility for the quality of a student's learning from his or her parent's shoulders. It has also removed some of that responsibility from the student's as well. The entire burden of this program rests solely on the shoulders of teachers. Any program that does not share the responsibility of education between teachers, parents, and students will falter or fail altogether. This simple old formula has been tested in this country for over a hundred years. It works, but it is very difficult to enforce. Such a plan—one that brings administrators, teachers, student, and parents into partnership in the quest for better education— is precisely the plan that a President (with a librarian as a wife no less!) should have proposed. It is the type of plan that you would have expected a President who talks about family values would support. What Mr Bush needs to add into his plans for improving the education of American children is methods of encouraging parents to get involved in their children's educational process. Once you can get the parents involved, *then* hold teachers accountable. Additionally, he should consider raising teachers' salaries, so that they are paid like the professionals that they are. Most importantly, devise a plan that helps students realize that, finally, they are the ones who are most responsible for their own learning. Mr. Bush should have used the Knowledge Is Power Program model. Only then will no child be left behind.

Chapter 4 –
The Economy, Tax Cuts and Jobs – The Shell game with your money and your job

In the 1992 presidential campaign Bill Clinton asked "are you better off now than you were four years ago?" In 2004, the debate will again be about the economy and jobs. Like Clinton before him, President George W. Bush 43 is staking his re-election on the economy and jobs. Jobs in particular will take center stage. The President has forced through Congress two major tax cuts, which, according to the White House's "Jobs and Economic Growth" document, will increase economic recovery and create many new jobs. The President's strategy is to supply businesses extra capital by eliminating the dividend tax; he hopes that these tax cuts will create incentives for small businesses, in particular, to grow and expand.

I am not an economist. I am a surgeon. Like all other Americans, I feel our tax laws are too complex; how many of us really understand how we are taxed and according to what principles? I suggest that some basic questions need to be asked about our system of taxation before we investigate our President's economic policy. Let's begin with a simple question: Is the tax system fair? While we might expect that those who have the highest incomes in our country would pay the highest taxes, in fact most of us believe that the rich have become not only very successful but also very creative at avoiding paying their fair share of taxes.

I don't understand all the ins and outs of our system, but there are a few things that I do know about taxes. First, they are necessary. I do not like writing that check to the IRS in April anymore than anyone else, but I understand that taxes make our incredibly comfortable way of life possible. Taxes are the membership dues we pay to belong to the country club called the United States of America. Everyone understands that the government cannot exist without tax revenue. Taxes go to pay for the military and the high tech F-22 Raptor with its precision guided weapons. Taxes go to pay for our highways, which are the best anywhere in the world. Taxes pay for the FBI, the CIA, the coast guard, and hundreds of other important agencies that keep our county safe. In the April 12, 2004, issue of *Newsweek*, Alan Sloan described the importance of taxes like this, "Not only are taxes going to be a central issue of the presidential campaign, but there are huge stakes here—nothing less than the financial well-being of our government and your family, not to mention of generations to come. It's not just about how much money you send to Washington (or get from it). Taxes are really a policy statement that reflects our government's notion of fairness..."

But the last words of Sloan's comment register what I consider to be a serious problem for us as citizens and voters: Do we really feel our tax system IS fair? Do most Americans feel as though THEY are the ones who have the final say about where our government spends our tax dollars?

As a nation we have to decide where to spend our money. What are our priorities? Do we need to be safer? Do we need to increase spending on our military and our intelligence services? Do we need to feed our hungry or house the homeless? Should we spend more money on education? Healthcare? Clearly the decisions about how the government spends our taxes should reflect the beliefs of the majority of our citizens.

To understand which decisions about spending will be the most beneficial in the long run, we must remind ourselves how our economy works. The economy is driven by spending, not corporate spending, but spending by you and me. In fact, consumer spending accounts for two-thirds of our economy. The key to fixing the economy lies in fixing the average American's pocketbook, that is, in giving Americans more money to pump into the economy. The question is what is the best way to give Joe Smith more money? Among the many economic theories attempting to answer this question, Democrats and Republicans focus upon two: decreasing the deficit in the nation's budget and cutting taxes. The Democrats favor decreasing the deficit, and they believe that increasing taxes on the wealthy will accomplish this and lead to a stronger economy. They theorize that interest rates will go down when the government debt is lower, and so money will be easier to borrow. More borrowing, they believe, equals more spending.

The Republicans favor cuttings taxes, particularly cutting taxes for the wealthy. This theory, in my opinion, predicts two outcomes: First, at the simplest level, by putting more money in the pockets of the wealthy, much *bigger* spending will take place, and this will help to stimulate the economy. Second, the wealthy will tend to grow their businesses, and this will lead to more jobs and more circulation of capital.

President Bush entered the White House and made a lot of promises to the American people. One of them was to tax cuts; he made this promise because he believes that even with these cuts, the government has "ample revenues to fund our priorities, to pay down debt, to set aside money for a contingency." Based upon this theory, our President proposed, and Congress granted, three tax cuts since he was elected in 2000. The questions we must all ask ourselves are: was he right? Did the tax cuts help the average American? Has our economy been truly stimulated?

President Bush was wrong. His math was wrong. The government did not have "ample revenues" to pay down the debt *and* give the people several huge tax cuts. Less than six months after passing his first tax plan, America was back in deficits. Let's do the math. In David Corn's book *The Lies of George W. Bush,* Corn, who is the

Washington editor of *The Nation* magazine, notes that the Center on Budget and Policy Priorities, a nonpartisan think tank, predicted that the tax cuts would remove up to $2.1 trillion over ten years from our national treasury. In late January of 2001 the Congressional Budget Office computed the national budget surplus would be $3.1 trillion in ten years. By this reckoning, then, there should have been one trillion dollars left over in the US budget. It did not work out that way. The estimates that the Congressional Budget Office used were flawed. They should not have been, but they were. The Center on Budget and Policy Priorities calculated the surplus to be only two trillion dollars. Therefore, enacting President Bush's tax cuts will eventually lead America's budget into a $100 billion deficit. Mr. Corn summed up this problem like this, "The White House underestimated the tax cuts by about a half a trillion dollars; it overestimated the surplus by about $1 trillion." The President stated clearly in January, 2001, "I think it helps further the case that there is enough money to pay down debt, to meet priorities, and to give some of the money back to the people who pay the bills." There was enough money, but he spent it in tax cuts.

Let's see how much the tax cuts helped Americans. Using some fictitious families and assuming each has only one breadwinner and no deductions besides those mentioned, here's how the tax cuts "helped" some average Americans. Kathy Joe Johnson is a staff nurse who is single, twenty-five years old, and works in an emergency room. She lives in the Midwest. She makes $44,000 per year. According to the Heritage Foundation's tax calculator, Kathy

Joe's tax cut will equal a whopping $206. This is a 3.4% tax cut. OK, maybe this is not the best example. Chris Smith is the fictitious nerd of whom we all made fun when we were growing up. He is now a computer programmer with a wife and two children. He makes $75,000 a year. Chris's tax cut is over $1,600. Steve West is a middle management hospital administrator. He is married and has two children. He takes home $200,000 per year. His tax cut is $2,916. Steve's younger brother, Fred, hasn't done as well financially. He only makes $25,000 a year. He is married and has four children. Using the same Heritage Foundation tax calculator, Fred West and his family, who are the ones in this group who need the most tax relief, get zero. They receive nothing from Bush's tax plan.

So Bush 43 went out to sell his tax cuts to America even before he was elected. He stated that, "The vast majority of my [proposed] tax cuts go to the bottom end of the spectrum," while he was on the campaign trail. If the tax cuts go to the bottom half of the economic ladder, then maybe the tax cuts will stimulate growth, increase jobs, and generate more income for the average American. Unfortunately, it does not look like this worked out as planned. (Although I find the phrase "bottom half of the economic ladder" troubling, Bush used it on several occasions, including while talking to the National Restaurant Association on April 2, 2001, and while speaking at the Kirkwood Community Center in St. Louis, Missouri, on February 20, 2001. So, I'll use it.) Did President Bush's tax cut go to the "bottom half of the economic ladder?" Not, according to the Center on Budget and Policy Priorities. They break it down. The bottom 60%

A Letter to America

of tax-paying Americans received only 13% of the tax cut revenue. Minorities are clearly at the "bottom half of the economic ladder." The tax cuts left out minorities completely. Fifty-three percent of Blacks and Hispanics got no tax relief. None.

Both Paul O'Neill, Secretary of the Treasury, and Alan Greenspan, Federal Reserve Chairman, worked behind the scenes with Congress to limit the size of the Bush tax cuts, because they thought the proposed cuts were reckless. Their efforts lessened the cuts somewhat. They were also the ones responsible for the instant stimulus which was the $300 or $600 rebate (Suskind).

The President played a type of shell game with the American people. He was talking about income tax and the lower half of the economic ladder. Americans who earn less than $35,000 per year pay almost nothing in income tax, but they do parcel out over $5,000 per year in payroll taxes such as Social Security, Medicare, etc. So, to cut the income tax of some one in this tax bracket means almost nothing. To help these Americans, the President needed to look under the other shell— the payroll tax shell. He didn't do this because he wanted to give tax breaks to the wealthy.

It seems that President Bush and his top advisers, including Larry Lindsey, the President's chief economic counsel, believed in Reagan era economics. Huge tax cuts were always the Reagan remedy. But the economy has changed since Reagan was in office. A large segment of the economy is now driven by high-tech computer software companies. It is unclear if these companies respond in the same manner as Exxon-Mobil, General Electric or General Motors to the implementation of economic policies of the past.

President Bush did get the economy moving in a positive direction. The tax cuts did infuse money into the economy. Money also flowed into the economy from the government, for his administration increased government spending massively. This guaranteed an increase in economic numbers. Let me repeat, this guaranteed good economic numbers.

We now have the information to answer several of questions asked earlier in this chapter. Did the tax cuts help the average American? The answer is clearly no. Did the tax cuts and increased government spending improve the economy? No. The purpose of stimulating economic growth should be to improve the lives of the average American. Our President failed in helping Joe Smith. I would argue that in spite of the excellent economic numbers the administration quotes us, we're still in trouble. We are in the middle of what has been called a "jobless" recovery. The numbers are sobering. According to the Economic Policy Institute, we are currently in the middle of the greatest sustained job-loss period since the great Depression. Between March 2001 and March 2003, the economy lost 2.4 million jobs. It has been estimated that another 2.4 million workers have also dropped out of the labor force. These are people who are not some actively seeking jobs because of frustration of not finding adequate work. Another 4.8 million workers are involuntarily working as part-timers because they're unable to find adequate full-time work. The White House promised 5.5 million jobs by the end of 2004. This rosy forecast was made by the White House's Council of Economic Advisers in May 2003. It does not seem that their estimate will be close.

The numbers are even worse when you factor in new workers. These are young people who have just reached the age at which they can work full time in careers, not just at jobs. From March 2001 until January 2004, the working age population in United States increased by 3.7% in. This was 222.7 million workers, compared to 214.5 million prior to 2001. In order for our economy to stay at a steady state, it has to create 2.8 million jobs every year. Large numbers of youth entering an economy that can no long accommodate them is a huge problem. It appears that economy has not even kept pace by generating the minimum jobs necessary to keep the unemployment rate steady. Forbes.com tracks the number of layoffs of over 2000 companies. So far this year as of July 10, 2004 over 51,000 people have been laid off. These are layoffs during a period of economic *growth*. Bank of America is laying off over 12,000 people. Du Pont is laying off over 2200 people. Sun Microsystems has shown over 3300 workers the door.

Here's the problem: companies have learned to do more with less for years. Wall Street has rewarded this handsomely. Corporate profits are high. Corporate cash flow is high. So why aren't corporations hiring? They don't need to hire. The corporate sector is not going to spur job growth. As long as corporations can do more with less, there is no reason to hire more workers. As long as corporate mergers continue, and they will, these mega-corporations will squeeze out middle management and the lowest men and women on the totem pole. This leaves workers no place to go.

The Bush administration has been less than honest with us about their economic and job policy. So, are we better off now than we were four years ago?

Chapter 5 –
Terrorism – A lot of running around but ...

In my lifetime there are some world events that I remember very clearly. January 28, 1986, is one of them. I was a third year medical student at the VA hospital in Dallas doing a psychiatric rotation, when one of the patients said that the Columbia had just blown up. I remember thinking that this patient was truly crazy. I went to the television, which is always on in the main room, and picture after picture of the shuttle exploding assaulted my brain. I loved space, astronomy, and NASA. I was heartbroken.

On April 19, 1995, I was the director of trauma at Louisiana State University Medical Center in Shreveport. I was in the emergency room seeing a patient, when a nurse informed me that there had just been a huge explosion in Oklahoma. Where in Oklahoma? Parts of Oklahoma were relatively close to Shreveport. Huge explosion?

How huge? Where? How was their trauma system going to be able to handle the patient load? What could I do? What could our trauma center do to help? After calling our hospital administrator and gathering more information on the exact nature of the tragedy, it was clear that there was not a lot that anyone at my hospital could do. Here I was, an experienced trauma surgeon, leading a Level 1, fully-equipped trauma center, and I could not do anything about the worst act of terrorism within our borders to date. I felt helpless. And angry.

On September 11, 2001, I was off duty with no clinical responsibilities. For a trauma surgeon, this usually means you are asleep. And, indeed, I was sleeping in after a long night on call in the ICU. The phone rang early that day. It was my wife's mother. We teasingly call her "The Town Crier," but she informs us of world events when we are too busy in the hospital to keep up. She called to say that something had happened in New York. A plane had hit one of the World Trade Center towers. In a sleepy fog, I turned on CNN. Nothing. Normal coverage. I turned on the radio next to the bed and listened to National Public Radio. Nothing. Normal coverage. I handed the phone to my wife, who was also sleeping, but I continued to surf the channels on our bedroom television, looking to see if my mother-in-law was right. She had to be mistaken. Then, on one of the news channels, it appeared, that unforgettable image we all saw of smoke pouring out of the North Tower. A couple of minutes later, CNN was on the story. I had it on the split screen, and there it stayed for the rest of the day. I watched events unfolding, just as the rest of our nation did. As I began to formulate explanations, for I knew, as Senator John McCain later said, that "pilots don't accidentally fly into buildings," the second plane hit. Watching that plane fly into the second tower, seeing the fiery explosion—all live—was one of those experiences that I am sure few of us will ever forget. Along with all the rest of America, I was sick and dumbfounded.

I called my partner, who was on call, and we discussed if there were anything we could do to help care for the sick and injured in New York. Our conclusion was not comforting. There was not much that we could offer, unless we flew to New York. We decided to wait and see how events developed.

Within an hour, it was clear that this was a terrorist attack on our—on *my*—homeland. Investigative reporters from every network were developing the story. It was a story of evil. A story of people who hated us so much that they had spent years planning and training for this horrible day. Over the next several days, weeks, and months, it became apparent that our way of life and our system were simply not prepared for such an audacious and vicious attack within our borders.

I had many questions. How did these terrorists get into our county? How did these thugs gain control of the planes? How could they hijack these planes without our knowing? How could we prevent the next attack, for surely, with the success of this one, others were likely to follow?

Currently, the 9-11 Commission is slowly, but I hope and believe thoroughly going through the mountains of information that might answer these and others questions about that fateful day. I hope and pray they will come up with recommendations to fix our system, so we will be protected against this kind of vicious insanity.

* * * *

To understand 9/11, it is useful to review the history of terrorism in or against the United States. Depending upon how you define terrorism, we have a number of events to consider. In her opening statement to the 9/11 Commission, National Security Advisor Condoleezza Rice mentioned the sinking of the Lusitania in 1915 as a terrorist act. Car and truck bombs seem to fit the definition of terrorism, too. In 1983 a truck bomb was driven into the US Marine barracks in Beirut, killing 278 of our Marines. Following the bombing of the Marine barracks in Beirut, we did not offer a significant military response. As a matter of fact, our government quietly withdrew the Marines from Beirut within a year after the bombing. But we might go back a little further and include the 1979 Iran hostage crisis, in which fifty-three Americans were held against their will for over a year. Our response to the Iran hostage crisis included a failed military rescue (remember the helicopters crashed in the desert?) and then a complex negotiation which included offering money and firearms in exchange for our hostages. In December of 1988, Pan Am flight 103 exploded over Lockerbie, Scotland. 259 people died in the tragedy. While people of many nations died in that explosion, most would agree that it was an attack aimed at the

A Letter to America

West, and especially at the US. It took authorities nearly three years to decide that this was a terrorist act planned in and sponsored by Libyans, not a freak accident. We mounted no military response against Libya. The most that was done, once it became clear what had happened, was that the first Bush administration imposed UN sanctions against Libya (all air travel to Libya was stopped, and all arms sales were halted). It took more than ten years of diplomacy before two suspects were finally tried before the World Court in the Netherlands and found guilty for the bombing of Pan Am 103 and the murder of 259 innocent souls.

Unfortunately, the recent history of terrorism doesn't stop with this court decision. During the Clinton administration, four major terrorist attacks took place: the bombing of our African embassies in 1998, which killed 250; the bombing of the World Trade Center garage in 1993, which took six lives and wounded over 1,000; the bombing of the Khobar Towers in 1996, which killed nineteen US soldiers; and the bombing of the USS Cole, which killed seventeen U.S. sailors.

Before this brief but horrific list of terrorist acts against our citizens causes too much discouragement, it is important to note that our government did begin to pay attention to terrorism during this time. President Clinton understood the threat. The 1993 World Trade Center bombing occurred only thirty-eight days after he took office. In mid-July of 1993 Clinton learned through intelligence sources that Iraq's Saddam Hussein had attempted to kill President George Herbert Walker Bush during his visit to Kuwait earlier in

1993. Clinton's response was to launch several cruise missiles at the Iraqi intelligence headquarters. Following the attack, Clinton stated on national television that we had retaliated against Iraq for their attempted assassination of our former President. Incredibly, according to the Counterterrorism Czar for Presidents Clinton and President George W. Bush 43, Richard Clarke, "subsequent to that June 1993 retaliation, the US intelligence and law enforcement communities never developed any evidence of further Iraqi support for terrorism directed against Americans." In June, 1995, President Clinton signed Presidential Decision Directive 39, which was a statement about US policy on counterterrorism. Claiming there would be no concessions to terrorists, the directive goes on to say, "The United States shall seek to deter terrorism through a clear public position that our policies will not be affected by terrorist acts and that we will act vigorously to deal with terrorists and their sponsors. Our actions will reduce the capabilities and support available to terrorists." According to Richard Clarke, after this directive was issued, counterterrorism funding increased from $5.7 billion in 1995 to $11.1 billion in 2000. Over that same time period, the FBI counterterrorism budget almost tripled. President Clinton used both of his crime bills to help increase funding for anti-terrorism measures. Because of this new focus, several terrorist plans were interrupted. According to a December 2000 article in the *Washington Post* al Qaeda had planned simultaneous bombings in the United States, Jordan, and Yemen, which were supposed to take place in January of 2000. Clinton's crime bills helped to foil these plots. After the bombings of the embassies in Tanzania and Kenya, which were also attributed to bin Laden's al Qaeda organization, President Clinton issued a presidential directive approving the assassination of Osama bin Laden. He also launched Tomahawk missiles into the Sudan and Afghanistan at targets that we believed were al Qaeda encampments. Since that missile attack, the Sudan, which now suffers from a huge humanitarian problem and ethnic infighting, has worked steadily to cooperate with our antiterrorism efforts. It appears that launching a few missiles may do more to persuade governments than we previously thought. While some may argue that Clinton didn't do anything to combat terrorism, this evidence suggests otherwise. Whether or not he did enough is still in question.

In the middle of President Clinton's second term, he directed a commission, the US Commission on National Security/21st-century, to study the problem of terrorism. The commission was co-chaired by former Democratic Senator Gary Hart and former Republican Senator Warren Rudman. Among its fourteen-member panel members were former UN ambassador Andrew Young, columnist and former editor of the *New York Times* Op-Ed page Leslie Gelb, and former Speaker of the House Newt Gingrich. This panel was bipartisan and experienced in national and world affairs. The Commission concluded over two year's worth of research in January of 2001 and handed over their 156 page report to the newly-elected President Bush 43. The report was called *Roadmap for National Security: Imperative for Change*.

The report was strongly worded. It recommended over fifty changes that could help us combat terrorist threats. The changes can be grouped into five areas:

1. Insuring the security of the American homeland
2. Recapitalizing on America's strengths in science and education
3. Redesigning key institutions of the Executive Branch
4. Overhauling the US government's military and civilian personnel systems
5. Reorganizing Congress's role in national security affairs

To further secure our homeland, the commission suggested formation of the National Homeland Security Agency. It also suggested reorganizing the government so that the Coast Guard, the Federal Emergency Management Agency (FEMA), the Border Patrol, and the Customs Service would be rolled into this new agency. The commission also recommended the formation of a new office – Assistant Secretary for Homeland Security. This new office would interact with the Department of Defense regarding all matters of safety for American citizens. The National Guard would be charged with Homeland Security as its primary focus, a responsibility that has always been spelled out in the Constitution, but which had not been taken very seriously in the past.

The commission report noted that "Americans are living off the economic and security benefits of the last three generations' investment in science and education, but we are now consuming capital. Our systems of basic scientific research and education are in serious crisis, while other countries are redoubling their efforts. In the next quarter century, we will likely see ourselves surpassed, and in relative decline, unless we make a conscious national commitment to maintain our edge." The commission concluded that for us to fight terrorism, it is imperative that the United States remain the leader in science and technology. Therefore, they suggested doubling of the federal research and development budget by the year 2010. They also suggested increasing the role of the President's Science Advisor to oversee these changes in education and educational funding. Finally, the commissioners asked Congress to institute a comprehensive funding program that would produce the needed professionals in science and engineering, professionals whose expertise might be focused upon detecting and combating terrorist activity here and abroad.

The commission made several other recommendations for the Executive Branch of government. First, it suggested that the National Security Advisor should concentrate more on *coordinating* rather than formulating policy for national security activities. It argued that formation of national security policy should be left to other White House staff. The commission also suggested that the Secretary of the Treasury should be named to the National Security Council. This would underscore the importance of economics in international security policy. They also recommended that the Secretary of State create an Office of Strategic Planning, Assistance, and Budget, which would fund counterterrorism efforts.

Regarding the Department of Defense, the Hart-Rudman Commission made a multitude of specific recommendations, all designed to streamline the bureaucracy and improve efficiency, so that the right information about illegal and terrorist plans could reach those who are empowered to act upon those threats. Recommendations included staff reductions of the Joint Chiefs of Staff and the Military Services and Regional Command Staff by 10 to 15%. This recommendation was not for a reduction in fighting men, but for a reduction in mid-level managers and to improve efficiency. The commission believed that this reduction could improve the flow of information. They also suggested that the "defense industrial base" be widened to include nontraditional commercial industries. Suggested reductions in paperwork and other red-tape impediments were also encouraged so that more small, high-tech firms might work with the Pentagon to help develop systems that would detect and combat terrorism. The report noted the speed of change in technology of Silicon Valley companies (every twelve to eighteen months) and compared that to the sluggish response of the military to change: it takes over nine years to develop weapons and weapons systems. The hope was to help the Pentagon become more responsive to the rapid change in communication systems throughout the world, especially those that are now being utilized by terrorists.

The commission also recommended that the treatment of US military personnel needs to improve in order to keep a fully qualified and highly motivated fighting force. The commission suggested several changes to help recruitment and retention of qualified personnel. They suggested enhancing the GI Bill, so that it truly pays for the median college tuition cost. Other suggested enhancements would improve the ability of service men and women to own their own homes and would improve their medical benefits. Interestingly, considering the prevailing belief today that our intelligence community has been slow and inefficient in its response to the terrorist threat, the commission maintained that the structure of the intelligence community was inherently sound and did not require change. They did recommend that the President "order the setting of the national intelligence priorities through National Security Council guidance to the Director of Central Intelligence." They also stressed the necessity for human intelligence gathering.

The commission urged that Congress's committee structure needs to be revamped in order to place more emphasis on terrorism and the intelligence community. This would make it possible for Congressional leaders to be better educated in matters of national security, so they could make better informed decisions about funding of counterterrorism weapons and forces. Closer coordination with the Executive branch, including the National Security Advisor, was also recommended, in order to improve anti-terrorism policy. Finally, the commission urged that it is imperative that Congressional leaders work more closely with the President in order to form more thoughtful and insightful national security and foreign policies. Such were the recommendations given to President Bush 43 by the

US Commission on National Security/21st century in January of 2001. Bush was only in office a of couple days when he received the report.

Recently, the President and his aides have gone to great lengths to point out that nothing could have been done, or that nothing *more* could have been done to prevent 9/11. Moreover, they insist that terrorism has been a top priority of this administration. But was/is it? Did they do everything possible to protect us against the 9/11 attack?

Consider the information about terrorism that was made available to President Bush prior to 9/11. In National Security Advisor Condoleezza Rice's opening statement to the 9/11 Commission, Dr. Rice explained that she met with George Tenet, Director of the CIA, to discuss national security issues during the transition between Mr. Bush's election and his inauguration. This would have been in December 2000 and January 2001. The President-elect was also present at some of these meetings. She stated that al Qaeda activities along with "a variety of other topics, including North Korea, Iraq, the Middle East and the Balkans" were discussed. From Richard Clarke's accounts, it appears that Clarke met with Secretary of State Colin Powell, Vice President Dick Cheney, NSA Condoleezza Rice, and others on more than one occasion before September 11, 2001. Bob Woodward's book, *Bush at War* confirms these meetings. During these meeting al Qaeda was described as a "tremendous threat." The transition team for national security was told that "there was no doubt that bin Laden was coming after the United States again... but it was not clear when, where or how." Bin Laden was ranked by the CIA as "one of the three top threats facing the United States." These statements are unambiguous.

So the new President took office after having been briefed specifically about terrorist threats by Clinton's aides. There were a lot of things happening before 9/11/2001. Unfortunately, none of them adequately addressed terrorism. Richard Clarke asked for a Cabinet-level meeting about terrorist intelligence on January 25th, but his request was put off. The President was personally briefed about the risks of terrorism by Hart and Rudman in January 2001. He received the Hart–Rudman Commission report by mid-February of the same year. But there was no visible response from the new administration. Senators began to draft legislation to protect citizens against possible terrorist attacks, using recommendations from the Hart –Rudman Commission. In March of 2001, Representative Thornberry (R-Tx) introduced the National Homeland Security Agency Act in the House of Representatives. Initially the White House opposed the idea of forming a Department of Homeland Security; of course later— *after* 9/11—that became a central plank in the President's war against terrorism. On April 30, 2001, Clarke, the White House's National Coordinator of Counterterrorism, presented a plan for how to eliminate al Qaeda. This plan was presented to the administration's deputies committee that included National Security Deputy Steve Hadley, Deputy Secretary of Defense Paul Wolfowitz, and CIA Deputy Director John McLaughlin, to name a few.) The Cabinet-level meeting that Richard Clarke originally requested back in January was still months away. President Bush announced his own plan to combat the terrorism problem in May, 2001. Surprisingly, however, this plan did not even mention the Hart–Rudman Commission. His proposal centered on the Federal Emergency Management Agency (FEMA). Simply, FEMA would coordinate our terrorism response. President Bush also announced that Vice President Cheney, who was already dealing with the nation's energy policy, would produce a comprehensive counterterrorism plan by October of 2001. In May 2001, Secretary of Defense Donald Rumsfeld announced his Missile Defense Shield Plan on *Meet the Press*. Missile Defense? This plan suggests the direction that the administration's thinking and planning was taking. No one yet seemed to have considered the possibility of an attack such as the 9/11 tragedy—and yet there was increasing evidence that just such an attempt might be made. Richard Clarke reports that "By late June, Tenet and I were convinced that a major series of attacks was about to come." There was increased intelligence traffic in the CIA. Threatening intelligence reports were pouring in from credible sources. In an article published in *US News & World Report*, April 5, 2004, Dr. Condoleezza Rice is quoted as saying "I don't think anybody would have predicted that these people would take an airplane and slam it into the World Trade Center... that they would try to use an airplane as a missile." But, in fact, the stream of intelligence about terrorist activities *did* include evidence that might have led wary authorities to consider this as a possibility. For example, though Ramzi Yousef, one of the masterminds of the first

World Trade Center bombing, just eluded capture by police in Manila, a considerable amount of data was found in his hideout—including plans to smuggle bombs onto airplanes that made a number of stops before arriving at their final destinations. Apparently Yousef's group planned to assemble the bombs in the planes' bathrooms and then to get off at one of the plane's layovers. Somewhere in the air after that stop, the bomb would blow the plane and all its passengers to bits in midair. Another report, written in 1999 by the National Intelligence Council (a division of the CIA which reports to the Director of Intelligence) included the following chilling statement: "Suicide bombers belonging to al Qaeda's Martyrdom Battalion could crash-land an aircraft packed with high explosives (C-4 and semtex) into the Pentagon, the headquarters of the Central Intelligence Agency, or the White House. Ramzi Yousef had planned to do this against the CIA headquarters."

In addition to these reports, which should have put airplane suicide attacks such as those that took place on Sept. 11, 2001, on the President's radar, there were other equally disturbing reports. These referred to small groups or cells of terrorists that had taken up residence in the US. Apparently some of the members of these cells were US citizens, or were registered aliens who had resided in or traveled to the US for years, and who were in positions to maintain a support structure for terrorists' acts. Other reports noted that these groups appeared to be carefully observing various federal buildings in New York. The same document that warned about terrorist cells inside the US, the August 6th Presidential Daily Briefing that Dr.

Rice recently discussed with the 9/11 Commission, was entitled, "Bin Laden Determined to Strike in the US." Strangely, Dr. Rice told the commission that this was an "historical" document, not a report of an imminent or even expected attack. That document goes on to say "A clandestine source said in 1998 that a Bin Ladin cell in New York was recruiting Muslim-American youth for attacks. We have not been able to corroborate some of the more sensational threat reporting, such as that from a ... [deleted portion] (portions of the memo are still classified and were deleted by the White House) service in 1998 saying that Bin Ladin wanted to hijack a US aircraft to gain the release of 'Blind Shaykh' 'Umar 'Abd al-Rahman and other US-held extremists. Nevertheless, FBI information since that time indicates patterns of suspicious activity in this country consistent with preparations for hijackings or other types of attacks."

There had even been warning in July of 2001, relayed by Italian authorities, that Bin Laden might have plans to use an airline to try to kill President Bush. Such reports hardly seem "merely historical." They seem to be terribly ominous and something the government should have been fervently tracking; and, more importantly, something for which the government should have been making protective contingency plans. The fact that reported threats were personally directed at our President seems to make action upon these "reports" all the more imperative. That President Bush did not think he, himself, was at risk suggests that no major player with the ear of the President had yet "gotten it" that these terrorists really, and truly, had/have it in for us and would/will stop at nothing, including suicide

A Letter to America

and the assassination of an American President. A final measure of just how clueless the Bush administration seemed to be is the report that when President Clinton and President Bush were officially changing power, Clinton spoke explicitly about top priorities that the new President would need to address. He offered the Mr. Bush a list of what he hoped would be his top national security priorities once he was in office. At the top of the list was Bin Laden. Items two through five were: the Israeli-Palestinian problem, North Korea, the difficulties between Pakistan and India, and Saddam Hussein. According to one report, Mr. Bush thanked Mr. Clinton, but said, "I think you've got your priorities wrong. I'm putting Saddam at the top of the list" (Moore). Reflecting the President's focus, not upon Bin Ladin and terrorism, but upon Iraq and Saddam, a few months into the new administration, his Deputy Secretary of Defense Paul Wolfowitz was quoted as saying, "Well, I just don't understand why we are beginning to talk about this one man, bin Laden... there are others that do [commit terrorism] as well, at least as much. Iraqi terrorism for example." (Clarke) This administration was clearly preoccupied with Iraq and not terrorism.

On September 4, 2001, the principal's meeting on terrorism that Richard Clarke had asked for almost nine months earlier finally occurred. A document was developed from this meeting that became National Security Presidential Directive # 9. Number nine? Eight more directives were more important than this? On September 9th Congress proposed an increase of $600 million in funding to anti-terrorism programs, taking money from missile defense. Donald

Rumsfeld wasn't happy that his missile defense program was being cut. As a matter of fact, he suggested that the President might veto this proposed increase in anti-terrorism funding. As we all know, two days later this country sustained the worse terrorist attack in history.

We must ask ourselves, in view of the evidence presented above if our new President really did do everything in his power to try to prevent 9/11? President Bush has said, "Had I known there was going to be an attack on America, I would've moved mountains to stop the attack." (*New York Times*, April 18, 2004). But he *did* know *something* was afoot. He *did* have indications that something involving airplanes and government buildings was being contemplated by our enemies. He *did* know that there were people in place within our borders to assist terrorists. Some analysts don't blame the President, but rather his advisors and the intelligence community. Certainly it is clear that both the FBI and the CIA need to ramp up their efforts to gather intelligence, to increase the number of agents who speak the languages of our biggest terrorist enemies, and to coordinate and share their information-gathering activities and results.

But, even so, why didn't our President act on the Hart–Rudman Commission report? Provisions for legislation such as the Department of Homeland Security and the Patriot Act, both of which were pushed through *after* 9/11 were clearly outlined in the Hart-Rudman Commission Report.

Condoleezza Rice's words, "I don't think anybody would have predicted that these people would take an airplane and slam it into the World Trade Center... that they would try to use an airplane as a missile," echo in my mind. Nobody could have predicted? As a matter of fact, not only should we have been able to predict this scenario, we should've planned for it. Hindsight is always 20/20. But it is clear that more could have been done in the days and weeks before September 11, 2001. Whether the attacks on the World Trade Center could have been avoided is uncertain, but it seems clear to me that the Bush administration could have done much more to protect us. Beefing up security at airports would've been a start. Reinforcing the cockpit doors of all airliners would have been simple and easy. Perhaps it took the WTC attacks, and now the resurgence of violence in Iraq, for America and America's leaders to realize the degree to which many in the Islamic world hate us and the lengths they will go to in order to harm us.

My question now is this: are we ready for the next attack? For I have no doubt there will be others. Are our airports truly secure? Is all luggage being effectively screened? What about our borders? Are they secure? We have thousands and thousands of miles of coastline and borders with Mexico and Canada. Illegal aliens across the border every day. Why can't terrorists? Several of the 9/11 terrorists were on the CIA's watch list, but the Department of Immigration and the FBI apparently knew nothing about them being in the country. Are the FBI's, CIA's, State Department's, Customs', and Immigration's computers integrated? Spain's transportation system has just been hit by terrorists. We have thousands of miles of railroad tracks in the United States, too. How often are our RR tracks checked for bombs? How well are these passengers screened? What about shipping and our sea ports? These are the questions the bother me, especially when our President says he is "doing all he can." My own experience as a traveler is that security still isn't tight enough to satisfy me.

Other questions rattle around in my mind. Although, we have chased the Taliban out of Afghanistan, what are we doing about other al Qaeda cells? We know they are operating in forty to fifty countries, including the Philippines, Indonesia, and Pakistan. Are we taking the fight to them all over the world? I am concerned that critical resources have been diverted away from the global fight against terrorism in order to finish the conflict in Iraq. This may leave our homeland vulnerable. I agree totally with Warren Rudman when he said (after 9/11), "… if two years go by and the same thing (September 11th type of attack) happens again, shame on everybody. I'm not pointing fingers. I just want to see some results."

Being a physician, the analogy that comes immediately to my mind to characterize our response to the threat of terrorism is a medical one. I am thinking of doctors who take a conservative approach when certain symptoms present themselves in a patient. Imagine if an obese man, in his mid-fifties, comes into my office and complains of nausea and arm pain with exertion. Suppose I perform a thorough physical examination and find, in addition to his obvious and life-threatening obesity, that the patient has a moderate amount of hypertension. Suppose I write him a scrip for xyz—a common anti-hypertension medication and schedule him for cardiac stress test in two weeks. My patient thanks me and leaves the office. Two days later I am called to the emergency room. Because I was conservative instead of aggressive, polite instead of tough, quiescent instead of proactive, my patient is lying on a gurney, struggling for his life after having sustained a massive heart attack. He showed me many of the warning signs of significant heart disease – arm pain with exertion, nausea from low blood flow to the abdomen and obesity. It is the responsibility of a physician to pick up on all of the clues our patients' bodies present to us. It is our responsibility to intervene quickly and appropriately to avert predictable health events that could have tragic consequences. It was the responsibility of our President and his administration not only to have picked up on the clues that evil might be afoot in our great land, but for them to have acted more aggressively and proactively to intervene on our behalf.

Chapter 6 –
The Axis: Name Calling – "You're evil."

My mother grew up in the ghettos of Baltimore in the 1930's and 1940's. It was tough then, as it is now. Diplomacy was an important part of survival. You cannot pick every fight, nor can you accept every fight and expect to survive. My mother has told me a thousand times, "If you can't say something nice about somebody, then don't say anything at all." As a young teenager, I felt that the phrase seemed a bit cliché. As a young adult, I began to appreciate its wisdom. Now, I cherish the phrase. Public denouncements and trash-talking should be reserved for computer-simulated combat. Some parents of prep school athletes and other sports fans might even come to appreciate that trash-talking is inappropriate on football and soccer fields as well as on basketball courts.

On January 29, 2002, President Bush delivered his first State of the Union address. Echoing a previous President, Ronald Reagan, Mr. Bush declared, "States like these (Iraq, Iran and North Korea), and their terrorist allies, constitute an axis of evil, arming to threaten the peace of the world." Hearing this statement, I thought of my mother and the lesson she learned growing up in Baltimore. Name calling in global politics is the same as doing it in Baltimore; but on a different scale, it is just as dangerous for the US today as it was for my mother in the 40's. So I wonder about Mr. Bush's strategy in making statements such as this. What can be gained by insulting loose and dangerous little cannons such as these three nations? 21st-century diplomacy calls for different and better strategies.

In the sandbox of the world, we are the biggest and the strongest kid. Hundreds of other nations play in this sandbox, too. As the lone surviving superpower, the US is the kid who has the ability to beat up or humiliate any of the other kids in this sandbox. The leaders of other nations in the world, such as Germany, England, Japan, and France, do not deliver "axis of evil" speeches. As the biggest and the strongest player in the sandbox, shouldn't it be our duty to make everyone feel welcome? Certainly it is apparent that it is incumbent upon our nation to lead the rest of the world and to help control the bad behavior of those nations that haven't yet learned how to operate in a global system. But you don't lead by taunting. To quote another Republican President, Dwight D. Eisenhower, "You do not lead by hitting people over the head—that's assault, not leadership."

In 1981, when President Reagan surprised (and possibly gratified) many Americans by calling the Soviet Union an "evil empire," there were two superpowers. Now there's only one. We cannot deny that the world dynamic has changed over the last twenty to thirty years. The difference in how our President must interact with and respond to the needs, initiatives, and misdeeds of other countries is enormous. As President Nixon said in *Beyond Peace*, "when the people of the world look at us, they should see not just our money and our arsenal, but also our vast capacity as a force for good." This "force for good" is vitally important, especially since so many people around the globe have come to hate us. We cannot speak or be perceived as the world's bully simply because we are the sole remaining superpower. Whatever you might think of Richard Nixon, he spoke good sense when he wrote, "we stand at a great watershed in history, looking back on a century of war and dictatorship and looking forward to a century (21st) we can make one of peace and freedom. The future beyond peace is in our hands."

When I look at the threats and opportunities of this new century, I see, as many Americans must, the threat to peace and freedom that seem to be coming from nations such as Iran, North Korea, Afghanistan, and—of course—Iraq. President Clinton attempted to confront some of these problems using diplomacy, not threats. And while he certainly didn't solve all the problems these nations present to the rest of the world, he didn't take us into a war that is beginning to look like another Vietnam and that seems to be inciting *more* anti-American sentiment around the globe than any of us want.

Let us briefly look at the history of these four countries (Iraq will be discussed in the following chapter). If we are able to understand their history, then perhaps we can make some sense of what is really happening over there. Perhaps we can think more insightfully about how we can or should deal with these countries and whether or not we think the foreign policies which President Bush has implemented to date are on the right track.

North Korea. After the Korean War, North Korea closely aligned itself with the Soviet Union, while South Korea became a strong ally of the United States. Over the next forty years, South Korea developed into a stable democracy with a thriving economy. North Korea developed into a brutal dictatorship, heavily reliant on the Soviet Union. But when the Soviet Union began to collapse in the late 1980's, the Soviets' promises of financial and military support for North Korea could no longer be met. Without the USSR's influence keeping the tyrants keeping North Korea in check, that nation quickly became a problem on the world's stage. In 1985 the North Koreans signed the Nuclear Nonproliferation Treaty (the treaty was originally drafted and agreed upon in 1969). But in 1989, North Korea nevertheless began to build its first nuclear reactor in Yongbyon. President Bush 41 chose quiet diplomacy to push North Korea into compliance with the Nuclear Nonproliferation Treaty. It took almost three years before North Korea allowed International Atomic Energy Association inspectors into the country, but this eventually happened in 1992. The inspection team was led by Hans Blix, who would later become famous for weapons inspections in Iraq. The IAEA inspection team met with many frustrations in North Korea. Access to important facilities were denied time and time again. Tensions escalated when one team found evidence of plutonium production—a clear indicator that North Korea was, indeed, violating the non-proliferation treaty it had signed seven years before. At that point North Korea threatened to pull out of the nonproliferation treaty. When President Clinton came into office later that year, he appointed a special envoy to begin significant negotiations with North Korea. This seemed to work, for in March of 1993 North Korea announced that they would not withdraw from the Nuclear Nonproliferation Treaty. But in April 1994, North Korea once again defied the international community by announcing that they were reprocessing spent fuel rods, which amounted to another step closer to making a nuclear bomb. President Clinton began to entertain military options, but his advisors' early estimates of over 100,000 casualties to American and Allied forces and over one million refuges persuaded him to continue with what were very difficult diplomatic efforts. We pressed for UN sanctions. South Korea began military exercises to prepare to defend herself from a possible North Korean invasion. In June 1994, despite some objections from the Clinton administration, former President Jimmy Carter visited North Korea and met with President Kim Il Sung. President Carter persuaded Kim Il Sung to return to the negotiating table. Carter also convinced the United States not to impose sanctions or to insist that the United Nations do the same. This was a major coup for American foreign policy. Less than a month later, Kim Il Sung died of a massive heart attack. His son, Kim Jong Il, ascended to power. Unfortunately, according to the State Department and the CIA, Kim Jong Il has been linked with several terrorist acts, including the bombing of a South Korean airliner in 1985, which took 115 lives. He is also thought to be the mastermind behind that nation's nuclear program. Despite all this, in October of 1994 an agreement was reached between North Korea and the Clinton administration. North Korea agreed to shut down its nuclear operations, and the United States agreed to help with the construction of two light water reactors to help North Korea with its energy needs. We also agreed to provide 500,000 metric tons of heavy fuel oil while the reactors were being built. In December of the same year, however, tensions between the US and North Korea were again strained when North Korea shot down an American helicopter, killing the pilot. The North Koreans claimed we had violated their airspace, and they suspected us of spying. North Korea, however, was hardly in a good position to move so aggressively against the US, for by 1995 governmental mismanagement, a lack of Soviet Union support, droughts, and floods had devastated the country. Reliable news sources report that between 1995 and 2000, an estimated two million North Koreans died of starvation.

In efforts to ease tensions between North Korea and the US, South Korea instituted what they called a "Sunshine Policy" in 1998. With strong support from the Clinton administration, South Korea attempted to engage North Korea in open dialogue. At long last, goodwill was building between the two bitter enemies. The world seemed to heave a big sigh of relief. But the goodwill was short lived. North Korea, a country that could not feed its own people, was pouring millions of dollars into missile technology. Worse still, in August of 1998, North Korea launched a long-range missile into the Sea of Japan, thereby proving that it now has the capability to strike Japan as well as South Korea. Intense negotiations began between the US and North Korea after this incident. North Korea finally agreed to allow United Nations inspectors into nuclear sites at Kumchangri in exchange for food aid.

William Perry, a former Secretary of Defense, was commissioned to study the United States' policy towards North Korea. His report stated, "The urgent focus of US policy towards the DPRK (Democratic People's Republic of Korea) must be to end its nuclear weapons and long-range missile related activities". (I'm sorry, I cannot resist this aside. Whenever a nation begins to call itself the Democratic People's Republic of X, Y or Z, you may be assured that their has nothing to do with democracy or the people. As a matter of fact, it is often the case that these "democratic" regimes are models of dictatorship, ruthless suppression, and single-minded quests for more power.) The next eighteen months seemed to promise an improvement in relations between North Korea and the US. North Korea pledged to freeze all tests of long-range missiles and to stop building its nuclear arsenal. Sanctioned by the US, Kim Dae Jung, the South Korean leader, traveled to North Korea for a summit with Kim Jong Il. This was the first time that a South Korean leader had traveled to North Korea since the end of the Korean War in 1953.

The summit appeared to highlight a change in North Korean foreign policy. For the first time in more than forty years the North Korean government allowed its citizens to visit South Korea. In the summer of 2000, families that had been separated for decades because of the partitioning of North and South Korea, held emotional reunions. In October of that same year, the highest ranking US official to visit North Korea since the Korean War, Secretary of State Madeleine Albright, landed in Pyongyang in order to speak directly to that nation's leaders. Several important issues were discussed, including their missile program and food shortages. After this meeting, North Korea invited President Clinton for an official visit—another diplomatic first. Unfortunately Mr. Clinton was so personally embroiled in trying to solve the Middle East conflict and so close to the end of his second term in office, this meeting never took place.

It seemed that diplomacy was working. North Korea had stopped making nuclear weapons. North Korea had opened its borders to its neighbor South Korea. Diplomacy had taken a bad situation and improved it for everyone (the South Koreans, the Japanese, and the Americans). My mother knew that being aggressive and posturing in a bad neighborhood was a bad policy. President Bush has never learned this lesson. Presidents Bush 41 and Clinton knew the value of diplomacy. They walked softly. Everyone knows the United States has a big stick. Unfortunately, Bush 43 ignored this history lesson.

After less than three months in office, President Bush began to undo ten years of relatively effective diplomatic negotiations with North Korea. First, during a meeting at the White House, he told

A Letter to America

the South Korean President that United States will discontinue all negotiations with North Korea. The South Korean President was stunned by this sudden development, one that indicates a major policy shift, a shift that has been initiated unilaterally, without even inviting South Korean input. Relations began to deteriorate between the United States and North Korea from that point forward. In 2001, President Bush declared in a public statement before the White House Press core in the Oral Office that he does not believe North Korea can be trusted. Hearing this, the North Koreans immediately threatened to restart their nuclear program. Later in 2001 the CIA reported evidence that North Korea has now begun a uranium enrichment program, which is in direct violation of the 1994 Agreed Framework. Then in January of 2002, Mr. Bush delivered his axis of evil speech. The "Sunshine Policy" is now officially dead.

Considering the instability of North Korea, this newly aggressive stance against North Korea is unlikely to make us safer. Richard Nixon—possibly one of our most astute specialists in foreign policy— stated over a decade ago that "We can not lead solely by example nor solely by power, but [we] must combine the best elements of both." It would seem that President George W. Bush 43 is ignoring this advice. He appears to think that physical power is his only resource in foreign policy. It would appear that President Bush 43 is trying to bring back Reagan era policy. Reagan took a strong, bold stance against the Soviet Union. And, at that time, when there were two world superpowers, the strategy worked. This will not work today. The dynamics of global power have changed. Our strategies must change as well.

Ironically, not only is such an "in-your-face" strategy unlikely to enhance our position with North Korea or with the rest of the world, the reality is that we cannot afford a war with North Korea. If we were to launch an attack against North Korea, North Korea has enough weapons to retaliate by striking at South Korea and Japan, two of our closest allies. There can be little doubt that some of their nuclear weapons would be deployed, causing hundreds, if not thousands, of casualties in South Korea and Japan. While we are so much stronger than North Korea militarily, we probably do not have the ability to destroy every single North Korean missile simultaneously. If we were to miss even one missile, thousands of civilians would die. Reality forces us to pursue diplomatic solutions. North Korea knows this. Surely our government knows this.

President Bush must engage North Korea with diplomacy. It seems to be the only reasonable course.

Afghanistan. Approximately the size of Texas, Afghanistan is an ancient land, ruled for centuries by the Persian Empire. It borders Iran to the west, the former Soviet Union republics to the north, and Pakistan to the east and south. A small portion of its border is shared with China and India. Evidence of ancient human civilizations in Afghanistan date back over 50,000 years.

Because of its proximity to Russia, China and India, the Soviet Union and the United States have been struggling to influence this region since the 1930's. In the 1950's the United States developed an alliance with the newly-formed nation of Pakistan causing Afghanistan to turn to the Soviet Union for protection. Prior to 1972 Afghanistan was ruled by a monarchy. Afghanistan has never had a royal family rule for more than a few decades. Since the 1700's, rulers were frequently toppled, another powerful family would ascend to the throne, only to be sacked by yet another group. Turmoil had always reigned in Afghanistan. Even during the rule of various monarchs, some inhabitants of the region belonged to the so-called People's Democratic Party of Afghanistan (PDPA), which actually adhered to Marxist, rather than democratic ideals. Moreover, it was a small party and did not represent the majority of the people of Afghanistan. Despite the possible stabilizing influence of various monarchs and/or Marxist ideologues, tribal infighting has prevented Afghanistan from progressing towards a more modern economy and standard of living. A full-fledged civil war broke out towards the end of 1979. It pitted the PDPA against Islamic extremists. In order to restore stability, the Soviet Union invaded with over 100,000 troops, easily captured the capital city of Kabul, and restored a certain degree of stability in the region. With the help of the Soviet Union, a new government (built from remnants of the PDPA) was put in place. This government, led by Babrak Karmal, however, began to crush all opposition. Prime Minister Karmal began arresting thousands of people. He used brutal military force, including aerial bombardment, to restore order. Hundreds of thousands of Afghans died during this period. Unwilling to sit by and watch this carnage, the United States, under Presidents Carter and Reagan, began to funnel money and weapons to a small resistance movement that had developed. This group, originally calling itself "jihad fighters" eventually became the "mujahedeen." The mujahedeen were a collection of Islamic organizations, which based themselves in Pakistan and Iran, both nations were at, that time, American allies. (Is this beginning to sound scary? It should.)

The mujahedeen resistance fighters were no match for the sophisticated army of the USSR. The armor-plated Russian helicopters were impervious to mujahedeen bullets and ruled the skies over Afghanistan. But soon, when we supplied them with American-made shoulder-launched Stinger missiles, the mujahedeen began to devastate the Russian helicopter fleet. Soviet casualties began to climb as the conflict dragged on for almost ten years. The Soviet Union seemed to have stumbled into its own Vietnam. Islamic extremists from all over the world, eager to take part in the fight against the USSR, gravitated to the region and joined the mujahedeen. Many of these radicals were trained in the art of guerrilla warfare by our own CIA agents. In 1988, while President Bush 41 was in office, the Soviet Union signed the Geneva Accords, in which the Soviet Union agreed to pull out of Afghanistan. By February of 1989 the Soviet Union had turned power in the region over to the mujahedeen.

Infighting again ensued and continued for the next four years, but neither the United States nor the Soviet Union had an interest in Afghanistan at that time. No financial aid from either of these two superpowers was funneled into the country. Kabul was being shelled almost continuously during the early 1990's. The countryside was broken up into small regions, which were ruled by local mujahedeen fighters, who soon became recognized as warlords.

As these warlords became more powerful and threatening, Pakistan began to take a serious interest in what was happening in Afghanistan. Pakistan understood that stability in this region was important to its own national interest. Moreover, Pakistan wanted to sell goods in Central Asia through a stable Afghanistan. In 1994 Mullah Mohammad Omar, an obscure leader who never granted interviews with reporters, came to prominence in Afghanistan. He led a group of like-minded individuals who were exhausted with the chaos in that country. Seeing Mohammad Omar as capable of stabilizing their neighbor, Pakistan began to funnel money into his organization. Mohammad Omar's group eventually evolved into the group we now know as the Taliban. The Taliban strictly enforces its conservative interpretation of the Koran. Men must wear long unshaved beards. Women are not allowed on the street in the company of any man other than their husbands or brothers. Schools for women were not permitted. Women were ordered to cover their bodies, head to toe, in burkas. Music and dancing were also banned. As the Taliban began to seize control of Kabul, in 1995, the ousted resistance movement who believed in a milder form of Islam retreated to the north of the country. This movement led by Ahmad Shah Massoud, known as a brilliant military leader who had the ability to bring warlords together to fight, began to call itself the Northern Alliance. The Northern alliance would, eventually, be supported by the United States, but for a time they were on their own.

Now, we have all the players in place except for one. Osama Bin Laden, the son of a wealthy Saudi construction family, who had been in Afghanistan in the mid-1980s helping to organize the mujahedeen, ironically, with the help of the United States, returned to Afghanistan in 1996. By that year, the US had become disenchanted with Bin Laden because he spoke out against our keeping troops in Saudi Arabia, protect the kingdom and the royal family from Iraq, after the 1991 Gulf War. Bin Laden ended up in Afghanistan because the US had insisted that the Sudanese government evict him from the refuge he'd taken in Khartoum. When the Taliban took control of Afghanistan in 1997, Bin Laden allied himself with the Taliban government. The country was renamed the Islamic Emirate of Afghanistan, a name signifying the Taliban's extreme interpretation of Islamic law.

Bin Laden hated the US. His hatred grew with every minute that the US troops were in his homeland of Saudi Arabia. He also violently disagreed with the American policy in Palestine. In 1998, Bin Laden called for all American and Jews to be killed. The CIA now believes Bin Laden's supporters, al Qaeda, acted upon their anger by supplying the Somalis who used hand-held rocket-propelled grenades against the US in the famous Black Hawk Down incident. Remember that the US left Somalia after this incident 6 months later. Bin Laden took credit for running a superpower out of Africa. He spoke of killing Americans until the US was complete out of the

Saudi Arabia. Mohammad Omar and the Taliban had no real foreign policy until Bin Laden suggested the "hate-America" policy. This policy proved to fit the Taliban perfectly.

Looking at the recent history of Afghanistan, it is clear how the United States' interest in the region waxed and waned; but it is also clear that such vacillation had a very negative effect upon those in power in the region such that they could plan the 9/11 attack upon New York City. Operating according to the old Cold War mentality (the enemy of my enemy is my friend), we embraced Muslim extremists—the mujahedeen— in order to oust the Soviet Union from this region. This was our first mistake. Under no circumstances should we have supported individuals adhering to this type of ideology; for, predictably, they radicalized—they became the Taliban— and grew hostile to the US. Had we kept hands off the region, it is likely that at least for a time the Soviet Union would have controlled Afghanistan. Then *they* would have become the hated outsiders that we have now become. We might have promoted democracy by supporting pro- Democratic revolutionaries inside Afghanistan. Once the USSR collapsed in the early 1990's, the US would have been in an ideal position to stabilize Afghanistan. Islamic extremists would have never gotten a toehold in the region. A pro-American democratic Islamic government could have been born, instead of the group that eventually planned and executed the 9/11 attack on the World Trade Center in NYC.

Our second mistake was to cut and run after the Soviet Union pulled out of Afghanistan, thus leaving a power vacuum in that region. This angered the mujahedeen, encouraged anti-American sentiment among its more radical factions, and probably contributed to the development of the Taliban, who have now become our sworn enemies. We had plenty of excuses for leaving those we had formerly supported in the lurch; in retrospect, none of them were good ones. But the reasoning went like this: The Cold War was over. Our foreign policy needed changing. In addition to this, Republicans in Congress wanted to cut foreign aid, especially to small "meaningless" countries. The attitude many expressed back in the 1990's was that the United States of America was no longer in the business of nation-building.

But none of these excuses seem adequate when they are compared to the events of September 11th. Of course, the United States of America did not fly planes into the World Trade Center and the Pentagon. Bin Laden and members of al Qaeda did. They are responsible. But the United States, so mis-handled the players in the volatile region of Afghanistan that we allowed an environment to develop that created the fanaticism of the Taliban. Because of this ineptitude—or, perhaps, arrogance –we contributed to the circumstances that led to the loss of over 3,000 souls in New York City on a sunny September morning.

After September 11th, the Bush Administration declared war on al Qaeda and the Taliban and began sending troops to Afghanistan. They made several critical mistakes in this War on Terror. We never committed enough troops to do the operation correctly. The purpose of the operation was to kill or capture the Taliban and al Qaeda. In order to achieve this goal, we needed to close off their backdoor. We needed to cut off escape routes to Pakistan. In our concern about avoiding American casualties, we never had enough troops in place to attempt to cut off the Eastern escape into Pakistan. At the beginning of the war, we were content to be the Air Force for the Northern Alliance. When we saw that this was going poorly, we committed more Special Forces. This drove the Taliban into the capital of Kabul. In *Bush at War* Bob Woodward points out the problem of not having adequate contacts or forces in the southern and eastern portion of Afghanistan. Almost all the leaders were allowed to escape into the friendly arms of Western Pakistan. Of the top fifty Taliban commanders, only four were captured or killed. The fierce fighting which took place in the Tora Bora Mountains was too little and too late. The Afghani troops, aided by our Special Forces, proved unable to take this rugged territory. With this military failure, Secretary of Defense Donald Rumsfeld announced that US forces would begin to take over the tough work. America, with the aid of our allies, should have been there in sufficient strength from the outset to do the job right the first time. Osama bin Laden and high-ranking members of the Taliban slipped out of Afghanistan while we waited for reinforcements. We had them cornered, but never had the troop strength to finish the job. Currently, there are more police officers in New York City then there are American troops in whole country of Afghanistan.

While it is true that al Qaeda is a remnant of its former self and The Taliban have been ousted from power, we still have to work to make sure that Afghanistan does not turn once again into a wasteland, where extremists and terrorists can take up residence and wage war against the West. The only way that we can prevent this outcome is through nation-building. We must learn from our mistakes in the recent past. Inaction and noninvolvement will produce fertile ground for extremists to flourish. We must avoid this at all costs. Out of the $87 Billion Iraq/Afghanistan Reconstruction package that was passed in Congress in November of 2003, only $1.2 billion has been set aside for Afghan reconstruction. The UN development program estimates that Afghanistan will require $7 to $12 billion over the next five years. We are underfunding the rebuilding of Afghanistan.

Some might suggest that I'm just an alarmist and that there is nothing to worry about in Afghanistan anymore. Perhaps the Taliban are nothing more than a bad memory. Well, recently fighting *has* broken out in several Afghani provinces (in October and again in December of 2003). Several aid agencies have scaled back operations in the area because of security concerns. Moreover, our troops stationed in the region are being attacked and killed once more by remnants of the Taliban and al Qaeda.

There is another concern about Afghanistan that many Americans seem to ignore. In the 1990's Afghanistan was one of the largest producers of opium in the world. Despite their many crimes, the Taliban did, at least, crush opium production by mid-2000. Poppy production is now on the rise again in Afghanistan. According to the UN, in 2004 approximately $2.3 billion will be generated by opium production in Afghanistan. This is approximately half of

Afghanistan's gross domestic product. We can hardly blame the poor Afghani farmers for their poppy crops. According to article in *The Washington Post* (November 10, 2003), growing poppies on a half acre of land usually yields over $1000, whereas growing wheat yields a paltry $70. This difference in profit, as well as the region's lack of infrastructure, such as irrigation, adequate roads, farming equipment, etc. make opium-growing a far more attractive crop than any other legal agricultural product. Here is an opportunity for America to intervene. If we could offer international aid to build infrastructure, help Afghani farmers find better ways to use their land, and encourage other ways of making good and honorable profits, we would not only be serving that nation, we would be serving the world.

The United States must build Afghanistan's infrastructure. We need to pour billions of dollars into their economy for roads, clean water, schools, communication networks, security, and investment and production alternatives to poppy growing. This is not something we *should* do; it is something we *must* do. We must support Afghanistan with the same enthusiasm that we supported Germany and Japan after World War II.

Iran. The geography of this is area somewhat confusing. Iraq borders Iran on the west. Afghanistan and Pakistan sit on Iran's eastern border. To the south are the Persian Gulf and Arabian Sea. To the north are several former Soviet Union republics.

Just about anything the Iranians have done in the past twenty five years qualifies them to be included in President Bush's "axis of evil" speech. We can go all the way back to the hostage crisis in 1979; but, instead, let's simply consider the Khobar tower bombings. In 1996, shortly after the Persian Gulf War, an American military unit was stationed in Saudi Arabia and quartered in the Khobar Towers in the Saudi capitol, Riyadh. Nineteen of our fellow countryman died in June of that year when a truck bomb was rammed into their barracks. The Saudi Hezbollah claimed immediate responsibility; and though Iran was never officially charged, it is clear Iranian fingerprints were all over this bombing. After over two years of stalling our attempts to investigate the Khobar tower bombing, the Saudis finally allowed the FBI to interview the suspects. The investigators were able to trace their activities directly back to the Iranian military. The Hezbollah were trained and funded by the Iranian Revolutionary Guard Corps' Qods Force, a standing branch of the Iranian military. This was no real surprise, for the Qods Force has sponsored terrorism throughout the region. Earlier in 1996, for example, a large mortar was seized in Belgium en route to Germany, perfect for lobbing over an embassy wall. This mortar was described as the "largest mortar ever seen," and it was traced back to Iran. In January of 2002 Israeli commandos stopped a ship in the Red Sea. The ship was carrying a large cache of explosives and was heading toward Palestine and Yasir Arafat. The ship was from Iran. Another reason to include Iran in the axis of evil is its apparent determination to create, and possibly use, weapons of mass destruction. We know that Iran has purchased technology from Russia to build a nuclear reactor. Iranian officials claim that the nuclear reactor is being built to meet this oil-rich country's growing energy needs; this is rather like saying you need to build an ice factory in Antarctica. The only reason to build a nuclear facility in Iran can be to create weapons of mass instruction. And, indeed, the International Atomic Energy Agency has found evidence that Iran is developing a nuclear weapons program. Pakistan already has nuclear capability. India also has nuclear capabilities. The possibility of another country in this unstable region obtaining nuclear weapons is chilling.

In addition to this record of international aggression, Iran also has a long history of civil rights abuses against its own citizens. Various humanitarian organizations as well as the US State Department have listed this nation on their watch lists for years. Their abuses appear to originate from a powerful group of Iranian religious clerics who, despite Iran's parliamentarian system of government, have ultimate power. They approve candidates before elections. They overturn court decisions. They run a brutal theocracy that has torture, false imprisonment, public floggings and executions without a trial.

While our diplomatic relations with this shady country have been very complicated in the past few decades, after September 11 we were able to exact a promise from Iran to close its borders to terrorists. To their credit, the Iranians have given humanitarian aid to Afghanistan. Unfortunately, they've also tried to influence the politics of Afghanistan by supplying weapons and money to several warlords who are hostile to the West.

We can have little doubt that Iranian officials are two-faced. On one hand, they have clearly stated that they would like to be our partners in the war against terrorism; but on the other hand, they have supported terrorism throughout the region. The question is what is the best way to confront Iran? Calling it names by lumping it together with the other bad actors in "the axis of evil," while tempting, does not seem to be the most constructive way of confronting this nation. Iran has acted as an enemy of peace and a friend to terrorists. This is a country that we should have dealt with forcefully—perhaps as forcefully as we have treated Iraq— demanding better behavior and threatening with military action.

The purpose of this review of the recent history of US involvement in North Korea, Afghanistan, and Iran, has been to highlight the problems with some of President Bush's most important foreign policy decisions. Former administrations had achieved a certain degree of success in dealing with North Korea using diplomacy rather than threats of force. By changing to more aggressive tactics, President Bush has only succeeded in provoking the North Koreans' quest for weapons of mass destruction.

Our meddling in Afghanistan, when the USSR was fighting there, allowed the wrong group to come to power—the Taliban, a group that is not only a humanitarian nightmare but also dedicated to attacking westerners, and especially Americans, whenever possible. When we, too, entered Afghanistan to fight, our purpose was not to liberate the Afghani people from an evil régime, but to kill or bring to justice those people who planned or helped to plan the events of September 11th. This goal was not accomplished. Osama bin Laden, many of his lieutenants, and most of the ranking members of the Taliban have eluded us.

As far as Iran goes, I believe President Bush has also blundered seriously. It is now clear that we have probably invaded the wrong country—Iran seems to be the most active sponsor of anti-Western terrorism in the Mideast. Iran is supporting the Palestinian Authority by shipping them arms in violation of international law. Iran has sponsored terrorism in Saudi Arabia. Their terrorist organizations have cells in Yemen, Saudi Arabia, Egypt, and probably many other countries, including Western ones. Iran, not Iraq, has always been the more imminent threat to the United States. There is nothing worse than the wrong war against the wrong foe at the wrong time.

Chapter 7 –
Iraq – Dorothy, we're not in Kansas any more

Compared to the US administration's handling of the difficult problems of North Korea, Iran, and Afghanistan, our handling of Iraq seems, well, rather crazy. By now it is pretty clear that Iraq had nothing to do, at least not directly, with the September 11 tragedy. Several of the hijackers were from Egypt and Saudi Arabia, but none were from Iraq. As a matter of fact, both the FBI and the CIA agree that there is no evidence of Iraqi terrorism since 1993. Richard Clarke argues this as well in his book, *Against All Enemies*. The fact that Iraq has been relatively inactive [before this war!] in the area of terrorism is probably a result of two policies. First: ten years of economic sanctions against Iraq were imposed by both the UN and the US. Second: The US bombed Iraq's intelligence headquarters with cruise missiles in 1993 after that nation foolishly made an attempt upon President Bush 41's life. Saddam seemed to get the messages from both the UN and the US loud and clear; and for almost ten years, we had no evidence of Iraqi complicity in international terrorism.

So why DID the second Bush administration go to war against this nation? Admittedly Iraq was lead by an evil tyrant, who committed enormous civil rights atrocities against his own people; but it is also a nation that was in economic ruins prior to our invasion? What was—what IS—the point?

In the 1991 Gulf War, Saddam invaded the sovereign nation of Kuwait. President Bush 41 gathered a large coalition of nations and, with the support of the United Nations, confronted Iraq. He was armed with the UN resolution which specifically empowered the coalition to remove Iraq from Kuwait. Therefore, it is not surprising that Bush gave the order to cease hostilities once the Iraqi forces were on the run out of Kuwait. Bush 41 been highly criticized for not taking the fight to Saddam, for not destroying him and his regime completely. Such action, however, was probably not justified. Bush 41's mandate was specific. It was to push Iraq out of Kuwait. Further military action would have caused fragmentation of the coalition. Many, if not all of the Arab nations (and quite possibly France, Germany, Russia and China) would most likely have pulled out of the coalition, if the United States chose to continue on to Baghdad. Such an act would have also removed the coalition's moral authority. In not pursuing the Iraqi army, Bush 41 followed his mandate and did the right thing at the time.

There are many issues worthy of debate with regard to the second US war with Iraq (Operation Iraqi Freedom), but I will limit myself to discussing the most recent military invasion, which began in March 20, 2002 and our subsequent occupation of Iraq. The United States made several errors before and during our initial invasion. The original invasion plans called for a three-pronged approach to conquering Iraq. We would fly in from the northeast across Turkey and drop troops. We would drive in from the south and split into two columns. One column would swing out through the desert in the west, while the other column would drive straight up the main highway toward Baghdad. All three of these forces would converge upon Iraq's capitol city. Our diplomats, however, were unable to procure permission for fly over rights from Turkey, this plan had to be scrapped.

Turkey's inflexibility meant our invasion forces were restricted to a one, or possibly two-pronged, assault from the south alone. Because the border with Iran, a country which we know supports terrorism, was not closed, Muslim extremists were able to stream in from the east. Indeed, a seemingly endless flood of terrorists was allowed to waltz into Iraq unimpeded by American or British forces. The presence of these fighters alone guarantees that peace in Iraq will be a long time coming.

Why didn't the allied forces plan for this contingency? Perhaps they simply misjudged Arab hostility toward the US and did not understand that our attack on Iraq gave anti-American extremists a perfect excuse to rise against us. Another reason had to be logistics:

In order for the United States to close and isolate Iraq from its neighbors, we would have had to commit more troops, tens of thousands more. The original invasion force during the Gulf War consisted of over 600,000 troops from many nations including Saudi Arabia, the United Kingdom, Qatar, Niger, Oman, Syria, Senegal, Kuwait, Morocco, Bahrain, Pakistan, the United Arab Emirates, France, Egypt, Bangladesh and of course, the US. Other countries (Spain, Italy, Czechoslovakia, Greece, Norway, Australia, Belgium, Denmark, Argentina, Portugal, Canada, New Zealand, the Netherlands, Poland, South Korea, Japan and Germany) provided ships, medical supplies and financial aid. The original invasion force in Operation Iraqi Freedom was only 150,000 which consisted of only British, Polish, Australian and American troops. There were not enough boots on the ground to close all of Iraq's borders. One US official in Bagdad characterized the problem like this, "there was a serious disconnect between the forces necessary to win a war and occupy a county. We fooled ourselves into thinking we would have a liberation over an occupation."

Another tactical miscalculation in our Iraqi Freedom campaign had to do with protecting our flanks. Iraq quickly figured out that our heavy armor would roll into town with guns blazing and would be virtually invincible. But Saddam also realized that our lightly armored vehicles would trail behind and that *these* troops *would* be vulnerable to his forces. Indeed, our lightly armored vehicles were sitting ducks for the Iraqis' rocket propelled grenades. It was a machine gun versus machine gun. This was much more of a fair

A Letter to America

fight. We needed more troops and more heavily armored vehicles to prevent Saddam's counter attacks. Following the fall of Baghdad, one does not need to be a military scholar in order to understand many of the problems that almost immediately ensued. Once we took the city, the local Iraqi police force evaporated. Imagine, if you will, a scenario in which all of the police in New York turn in their badges and go home. Chaos would ensue, as it did in Baghdad. The State Department had planned for this—led by a former general, Colin Powell—contingency, but the State Department was shut out by the Department of Defense—led by a businessman/bureaucrat, Donald Rumsfeld— and the White House, which gave the State Department no role in Iraq. The Department of Defense, in its Rumsfeldian arrogance, had not considered the possibility that the Iraqi police force might dissolve. So, for over two weeks there was looting and rioting in the streets of Baghdad— civil violence added to the military's burden. A terrible brew. Almost instantly, the United States lost credibility with the Iraqi man in the street, the one who originally supported our invasion. Donald Rumsfeld's response to this miserable situation, while technically accurate, did little to help the situation: "Freedom's untidy," he told the international press, "and free people are free to make mistakes and commit crimes and do bad things. They're also free to live their lives and do wonderful things. And that's what's going to happen here." The simple truth is, however, that our planners had miscalculated the effects of our invasion; and so there was another dimension of violence in Iraq: everyone from the smallest street vendor to the curators of Iraq's national museum had to protect what little wealth remained in the country from its own citizens. Not only were many small business people of Iraq devastated, but many of the country's priceless works of art disappeared or were destroyed. None of this improved our relations with the people whom we had come to "liberate."

The Defense Department also failed to plan for the decrepit state of Iraq's infrastructure. The roads, the water supply, the communications networks, and the oil fields had all been compromised by ten years of economic sanctions, the Persian Gulf War and the DOD's latest invasion. What little money that had been flowing into the country prior to our invasion was regularly pocketed by Saddam Hussein and his family. Not only this, but the nation's electrical grid and the water supply were sabotaged before the allies could take control of the country. Looking at the situation from the outside, it would appear that the United States had not planned for these problems. It took over two months for us to repair the electrical grid alone. Furthermore, the United States had planned on using revenue from newly captured Iraqi oil fields to pay for infrastructure repairs. Unfortunately, the Iraqi oil fields needed repairs themselves. The equipment was old and dysfunctional. Some industry experts estimate that it will take over five years to rebuild the Iraqi oil fields. Estimates of what it will cost to rebuild the rest of the country top $1.6 trillion over ten years. The failure to anticipate problems such as these, and the time it took for the allies to respond to some of these problems, led to more American and Iraqi deaths and to an intensification of the growing ill-will of Iraqi citizens toward America and our allies.

In addition to these problems, less than six weeks after the cessation of hostilities in Iraq, our head man on the ground, United States envoy Paul Bremmer, disbanded the Iraqi army. Thousands of men with weapons and ammunition were put out of work. A large fighting force which could have been used to help rebuild infrastructure, keep the peace, and distribute humanitarian aid was sent home. Moreover, the status and dignity of this once proud army were stripped from its members. If a portion of these men had supported the American cause—and we have every indication that many of them did— their minds were changed by Bremmer's decision. As the old Chinese proverb says, "keep your friends close and your enemies closer." If we had kept the Iraqi army intact and functional, but under Allied supervision, it would have been easier to watch for those who have since taken to skirmishing with and sniping at our troops. But we could have also paid them to rebuild roads, schools, and hospitals. This would have given them important humanitarian work to do for their countrymen; it would have restored a measure of their dignity; and it would have prevented many subsequent problems that have cost us money and lives.

Besides disbanding the Iraqi army, Bremmer removed all Baathist bureaucrats from their positions in the post-war administration of the country. Saddam's Baath party had ruled Iraq for over thirty years. Party members held all key positions in the government and in most civil agencies. By removing these people, Bremmer put almost every one of substance and experience out of work. The situation is reminiscent of the situation in Germany after World War II. Despite a worldwide call for the ouster of all Nazis, many allied leaders, generals, and administrators on the ground quickly learned that they needed certain Nazi specialists to help them keep what was left of Germany functioning. Bremmer and other administration officials seemed to have forgotten that lesson from the past.

No one should be surprised at the confusion and chaos that reigns in Iraq today. The police have gone home. The army has been disbanded. The government was completely fired. We have trained new Iraqi police force who are ill equipped to stand up to car bombs and well armed terrorists. Fighting in Najaf is that prime example. A police station was overrun by forces loyal to radical Shiite cleric Muqtada al-Sadr. After several days of heavy fighting, American forces were able to turn control of the city back over to the newly trained police force. Fallujah continues to be a security problem. There are kidnappings and beheadings almost weekly. There are few people who are familiar with the local infrastructure situations still in place to help run things, and few Iraqis have been tapped to help the allied forces keep order. The United States military is now responsible for everything. People who are trained in the art of war now are required to run a country and keep the peace. It is not the military's fault that things have been bumpy; they were never trained for this kind of duty. They are learning on-the-job.

Any decent military historian can tell you it takes more men to occupy a country than it does to conquer it. Yet, for months, as the violence in Iraq has re-escalated, the White House has resisted on *not* sending more men to Iraq. Only now, after a year of fighting and the loss of more than five hundred American soldiers' lives, has the White House requested more troops for Iraq.

On June 28, 2004, in a simple ceremony, the United States turned over sovereignty to the interim Iraqi government. President Bush has been asked several times just exactly what "turning over sovereignty" means. He has invaded the question. If he cannot answer the question then who can? One thing is clear, there will be more bombings and more kidnappings before this is all over.

All of this is regrettable. The way we have "conquered" Iraq has only played into the hands of the Muslim extremists and has probably made this a far more dangerous world for Westerners. Because of our own blunders—and some bad luck— Iraqi reconstruction has become a far more difficult job than we expected. It will take years for us to get Iraq on its feet again. We have lost our momentum in that country and much of the good will of the Iraqi people. Perhaps this is not another Vietnam, but it has certainly turned out to be a first class quagmire. It will take thoughtful, intelligent, and innovative men and women not only to rebuild Iraq, but also to pull the United States out of this mess and to restore our credibility and honor among nations around the world. Now that it is clear that American and Allied occupational forces will be in Iraq a lot longer than we had hoped, despite the "turn over" to the Iraqi provisional government, we must demonstrate to all Iraqis and to the Muslim world that we can be—that we *ARE*—a force for good.

Chapter 8 –
Religion - See no evil, Hear no evil.

Is it possible to be a good, strong leader and also be a Christian? To be a good Christian requires a love of God and love of your fellow man. Though not a Christian, Sun Tzu aptly described the characteristics of a good leader in *The Art of War*; he said a leader must be wise, sincere, benevolent, brave, and strict. A good Christian can certainly manifest these qualities of character as well. Our founding fathers, for example, had these characteristics. There are several examples of modern-day politicians who are both strong leaders and are very religious.

Separation of Church and State has been a tradition in this country since the days of the founding fathers. But in recent years, more and more Americans—including our political leaders—have been more vocal about their religious beliefs. Few have been more forthcoming on this issue than President George W. Bush 43. Indeed, it would seem at times that this president wears his religion on his sleeve. He has done more than court the Christian right for political purposes, he openly infuses religion into speeches and every day White House life. Cabinet meetings begin with a prayer. Following the lead of another President, Ronald Reagan, who spoke openly about his faith in God, Mr. Bush closes all his speeches with "God bless America." Mr. Bush has told us that he was in a Bible study group and that his faith in God plays a central role in his personal life. Religion in America is usually a private affair; but if the President is going to make his being a Christian an issue, then I believe it is important for us to examine his actions to see if they are, indeed, Christian.

We must remember that no one, no person, is a perfect Christian. We all have faults and flaws. These make us human, but the goal of all Christians is to behave as Christ did. This includes many things, but above all love for one's fellow man and compassion for all. Being a Christian must be seen in actions and not just words. In an episode of the popular television program, *The West Wing*, the drama's President, Josiah Bartlet, tries to determine if a Chinese refugee is really a Christian, and therefore worthy of asylum in the United States, or a fraud who needs to be shipped back to China. After the Chinese scientist answers several of Bartlett's questions he states, "Mr. President, Christianity is not demonstrated through a recitation of facts. You're seeking evidence of faith, a wholehearted acceptance of God's promise of a better world. For we hold that man is justified by faith alone is what St. Paul said. Justified by faith alone. Faith is the true…I'm trying to…(he searches for the right word) shibboleth. Faith is the true shibboleth." In other words, faith is the only true measure of a Christian. This was an astute response. If we apply this standard to President Bush, who has, indeed, recited a number of facts about his religious life, we must ask ourselves, do his *actions* demonstrate whole-hearted acceptance of God's promise? Does Mr. Bush show evidence of faith such as that described in Ephesians 3:17: "That Christ may dwell in your hearts by faith; [and that you are] rooted and grounded in love".

In the past several years, circumstances both in our country and abroad have provided a Christian President opportunities to demonstrate faith in action. For example, the Catholic Church has been rocked by scandals. Priests abusing children. Priests abusing young women. At first it seemed the problem was localized in Boston. But, as Johanna McGeary wrote in *Time Magazine*, it became clear that this problem persists "not just in Boston, but in Los Angeles, and St. Louis, Mo., and Philadelphia, and Palm Beach, Fla., and Washington and Portland, Maine, and Bridgeport, Conn." More and more victims of sexual abuse by a clergyman have come forward. At present, the Catholic Church appears to be trying to resist reality. Spokesmen for various dioceses have denied there is a serious problem, suggesting that these cases were isolated; there were only one or two bad apples among their priesthood. Unfortunately, "the crisis gather[ed] steam day after day, with perhaps 2,000 priests accused of abuse across the country and hot lines jam[med] with more victims' calls." Any religious person could see that there was a problem—a systemic, uniquely American problem—in the Catholic Church. As this crisis unfolded, it would have been an excellent time for a religious President to speak out, for though he is not a Catholic, he *is* a Christian. But President Bush remained silent.

The President was also silent when Catholic Bishop Thomas O'Brien, of Phoenix, Arizona, who had been acquitted of covering up priest abuse of children in June, 2002, was involved less than two weeks later in a fatal hit and run incident. He was driving. All of us are fallible. Accidents—even one so serious as running down another human being—while horrible, happen. But for a so-called "man of God" not to stop and render aid is criminal. At the very least O'Brien needed to call 911. He did neither. He hid at home until the police tracked him and his car down. A Christian man could easily see the harm that this Bishop had done to himself, his Church, and his community. Considering the growing crisis for the all churches in America, it would make sense that our Christian President might have at least commented upon this situation, that he might have tried to calm the uneasy and to remind our citizens that bad actors in whatever church can not fundamentally alter one's faith in God. But the President remained silent.

Another situation in which our avowedly Christian President appears to have failed to act in a Christian manner is in the treatment of the terrorists captured after the 9/11 attack on America. The US government removed these individuals from their homeland and brought them to Cuba for interrogation. These captured prisoners were reclassified as "unlawful combatants." At first I did not understand why the Bush Administration would go to the trouble of applying a new name for people who were obviously prisoners of war. Slowly, it dawned upon me. Our administration was trying to get around the Geneva Convention, which mandates humane treatment of all prisoners of war. These "unlawful combatants"—many of whom may be entirely innocent—are being held without even the basic rights that we gave Timothy McVeigh, who killed hundreds of our fellow Americans. These individuals have not been allowed access to lawyers. They have not experienced due process. It appears that we may hold some of these combatants indefinitely. Why would a Christian President allow his administration to circumvent the Geneva Convention in this way? Compassion, even and especially, towards our enemies is urged throughout the Bible. Consider the well-known story of the Good Samaritan told in Luke 10:30-36 "And Jesus answering said, A certain man went down from Jerusalem to Jericho, and fell among thieves, which stripped him of his raiment, and wounded him, and departed, leaving him half dead. And by chance there came down a certain priest that way: and when he saw him, he passed by on the other side. And likewise a Levite, when he was at the place, came and looked on him, and passed by on the other side. But a certain Samaritan, as he journeyed, came where he was: and when he saw him, he had compassion on him, and went to him, and bound up his wounds, pouring in oil and wine, and set him on his own beast, and brought him to an inn, and took care of him. And on the morrow when he departed, he took out two pence, and gave them to the host, and said unto him, Take care of him; and whatsoever thou spendest more, when I come again, I will repay thee. Which now of these three, thinkest thou, was neighbour unto him that fell among the thieves?" Also consider how Jesus behaved toward his persecutors. Where are the *actions* we might expect from a Christian leader with regard to the people imprisoned at Guantanamo? Are political expedients—the desire of American's for (unchristian) revenge after 9/11—outweighing Mr. Bush's duties as a man of God?

Does Mr. Bush merely speak words about faith without acting in accordance with that faith?

In May of 2004, the country began to be aware of the atrocities some of our service people were committing in the Abu Ghraib prison in Iraq. Truly abhorrent pictures were released by CBS News on April 27, 2004. Since that time Secretary of State Colin Powell, Secretary of Defense Donald Rumsfeld, and President Bush have all made clear statements denouncing this behavior. The Senate Armed Forces Committee immediately held hearings to investigate exactly what went wrong. More and more investigation reveals that the initial seven soldiers accused of torture are only the tip of the iceberg. In an article published in the *New Yorker* on May 24, 2004, Seymour Hersh states that Secretary of Defense Donald Rumsfeld developed a secret operation in Afghanistan to bypass red tape. It was thought that the United States had missed several opportunities to eliminate or capture high-level Taliban officials because of the need for prior approval before engaging them. (Our Armed Forces needed to get clearance from Washington before engaging a target.)

Therefore, a secret program was developed and "given blanket advance approval to kill or capture and, if possible, interrogate high-value targets." A different, but related story appeared in *Newsweek* (May 24, 2004) entitled, "The Roots Of Torture," suggesting that the behavior in Abu Ghraib is more than a failure of discipline, that it is a failure of policy—the same policy that Rumsfeld developed for Taliban prisoners from Afghanistan now in prison at Guantánamo. This story outlines the significant legal maneuvering that the Bush administration undertook to circumvent the Geneva Convention, as discussed above. Now it appears that procedures that were meant specifically for al Qaeda and the Taliban prisoners have now been used as well in Iraq.

We are at war, fighting an enemy that has no rule book. This is an enemy that will blow up a school bus full of children, if such an act will achieve their purposes. They are evil and relentless. But we are the United States of America. We are not only large and powerful, we are also the Home of the Free. We have "In God We Trust" inscribed on our currency. We have a President who is more outspokenly Christian than any in our history. Moreover, we entered this war on terrorism and the conflict in Iraq on moral high ground. We cannot and we should not relinquish it. I challenge Mr. Bush to look into his heart, to pray about our nation's recent actions, and to consider acting in a more thoroughly Christian way, even as we wage this terrible war against terror.

Besides my concerns about what I fear are failures of President Bush to act according to Christian principles, I also wonder about his humility, another Christian virtue. In the film *The Last Crusade*, one of the *Raiders of the Lost Ark* series, Indiana Jones finds himself in trouble again. His father is dying from a gunshot wound. He has to find the Holy Grail, the cup that Christ drank from at the Last Supper. He must get the cup and use its healing power to cure his dying father. There are three tests which Indiana Jones has to pass in order to get to the Grail. Many men have failed in this quest, as evidenced by all the skeletons on the ground at Indy's feet. But Jones is focused on his task. He is trying to figure out the riddle — "Only the penitent man shall pass." He is repeating this phrase over and over. Suddenly, the answer comes to him as he says, "the penitent man is humble before God." He falls to his knees just as a large saw blade slices the air above his bowed head. Has President Bush been humble? There are several examples of his recent behavior that suggest the answer is "no." Our complete and sudden reversal on American foreign policy towards North Korea without consultation with South Korea or Japan could easily be seen as arrogant. After dismantling the Taliban in Afghanistan, the Bush administration turned its attention to Iraq without regard to the strong objections of France, Germany and Russia. We told the world that we would go it alone, if we needed to, because this was vital to our national security. Boldness or arrogance?

The Judeo-Christian heritage teaches kindness to the poor and aid to the sick and elderly. A major tax relief package which gives almost no relief to Americans making less than $40,000 a year would seem to contradict this heritage. The new Medicare drug benefit program is targeted for the sick and elderly. Unfortunately, it is so complex that no one truly understands it. Its benefit to the elderly and poor is questionable.

"Jesus said unto him, Thou shalt love the Lord thy God with all thy heart, and with all thy soul, and with all thy mind. This is the first and great commandment. And the second is like unto it, Thou shalt love thy neighbour as thyself," (Matthew 22:37-39). This is the essence of Christianity. Love. A man's love for his God is personal and complex. A man's love for his neighbor is demonstrated through acts of kindness, compassion and humility. A President has hundreds of opportunities to demonstrate his love for his fellow man. There are millions of Americans who go to bed hungry at night. All they need is a helping hand from our government. There are millions of Americans who work on the assembly line performing crippling work minute after minute, hour after hour, day after day, year after year. All they need are some government regulations to help them do the work without permanently injuring themselves. Millions of Americans cannot afford health insurance. All they need is a little help from our government. Nearly every week a multibillion-dollar company, making record profits, lays off workers to improve their bottom-line. All these workers need is a little support from our government in order to earn a decent wage. Our elementary, junior high, and high schools are crumbling under the burden of underfunding. Our children are accosted everyday with drugs, sex, and violence in our public schools. All our educators need is presidential leadership and innovative funding. Education is the only consistent way out of poverty. Yet, state legislatures slash funding for higher education in order to balance state budgets. Lower class and middle class students are being priced out of college. These diligent citizens need help from our government. The heroes of September 11th, the police and fire departments, are being stretched beyond expectations. They are understaffed and overworked. They have had to carry the excess burden during this time of heightened security. Adequate funding was promised. All these good Americans need is for our government to live up to its promise. A President has the power to fix some, if not all of these problems, especially if he understands himself to be a servant of God. Unfortunately, in the Bush administration, many of these problems have gone unaddressed.

It is not my place or my desire to belittle our President's religious beliefs. I will not pass judgment on his beliefs. I have, however, highlighted some of his actions (and his failure to act) that seem to go directly against the teachings of Jesus Christ, teachings Mr. Bush says he embraces. President Bush does not seem to embrace the ideals of Christianity, at least not in his public life. "But thou, O man of God, flee these things; and follow after righteousness, godliness, faith, love, patience, meekness. Fight the good fight of faith, lay hold on eternal life, whereunto thou art also called, and hast professed a good profession before many witnesses. (1 Timothy 6:11-12)"

Chapter 9 –
Environment - please pass me a gas mask

I am no outdoorsman, but I have an appreciation for nature. I understand nature's importance in our lives, even if I'm not out backpacking in Big Bend National Park every weekend. As a child who grew up in the 60's, I have seen or read about the devastation that pollution can do to a river or community. In the early 60's, for example, Lake Erie was so filthy that parents would not let their children go near the lake, let alone swim in it. Rivers and streams in industrial areas have been known to ignite spontaneously because of the reckless way many industries have treated the land and water surrounding their factories. As a physician, I have seen far too many patients with birth defects, chronic lung diseases, and cancers that developed because certain corporations in this nation have not considered their impact upon our environment. Wall Street rewards companies for profits, not for looking out for the environment. As they grab for increased profits, many corporations have abdicated their social responsibility toward preserving a safe environment for our citizens.

Over the past thirty years, however, citizens and lawmakers have come to appreciate the importance of being more respectful of our environment. Through consistent governmental intervention, the United States has done much to improve degraded areas in our environment, to clean up rivers, and to clean up the air. More needs to be done; for one thing, our government needs to structure environmental and tax law so that industries whose production processes are most likely to pollute the environment will be *less* profitable if they do. It is within the power of the Presidency to make it clear to big businesses that cleaning up, or better yet, preserving and protecting our environment and all its wonderful natural resources is in their best interests.

An Environmental Defense poll performed in 2000 revealed the vast majority of Americans believe that the environment is getting worse. Over 65% of those polled expressed the belief that improved federal regulation was necessary and that they were ready to okay the use of federal dollars to protect the environment. In the same year, as he campaigned for the Presidency, George W. Bush 43 seemed to appreciate the findings of this poll, and he made several important promises in this regard. He promised that he would regulate carbon dioxide emissions. He noted during the presidential debates that "global warming needs to be taken seriously." Mr. Bush took on Al Gore, who has been deeply committed to environmental protectionism for years, by calling for mandatory reductions in industrial production of sulfur dioxide, nitrogen oxide, mercury and carbon dioxide. The Kyoto agreements are the UN sponsored initiative which requires thirty-eight industrial nations to reduce greenhouse gases by 5.2 percent below 1990 levels by the year 2012. This agreement has been signed by over 180 nations. But appeared from Bush 43's seemingly pro-environment rhetoric, that he might sign the document, which so many other nations had ratified and which is designed to reduce carbon-based emissions.

Despite all this, if the national media had examined Governor Bush's record on the environment in Texas, they would have seen an interesting pattern. Bush *talked* pro-environment but he *acted* pro-industry, including industries that are some of the worst of our polluters. Consider this: Texas has a terrible problem with air pollution. Houston, Dallas and San Antonio are among the most polluted cities in the US. Governor Bush's response was Senate Bill 766, an emissions-control bill. But not only did the bill merely urge *voluntary* emissions control on the part of industry, Mr. Bush allowed it to be drafted by R. Kinnan Goleman, who was at that time serving as chief counsel to the Texas Chemical Council. Governor Bush allowed an industry lobbyist to draft one of the most important environmental policy bills needed in the state of Texas. In addition to this, the bill was developed behind closed doors. No public forums. No legislative discussions. Governor Bush sent the bill to the Texas legislature audaciously claiming that this was a major step forward in cleaning up the environment that simultaneously avoided hamstringing industry. The popular Governor slid the bill through the Texas house and senate without much debate in May 1999. A year after the bill took effect, the Texas Natural Resource Conservation Commission found that this bill had achieved absolutely nothing towards the goal of cleaning up the state's environment. The Texas State Legislature rescinded the bill in the very next legislative session.

Fast forward to 2001, Governor Bush is now President Bush. Consider his actions on the part of the environment as the Chief Executive. First, he chose Christine Todd Whitman to head the EPA. Although Whitman had been the governor of New Jersey and had met Governor Bush on several occasions, she had never spoken with him about environmental policy. She presented herself as a moderate Republican and seemed to champion certain environmental issues, such as cleaning up the beaches and air in New Jersey. During her governorship there was a significant decrease of bad ozone days from forty-five to four. Her environmental efforts earned her praise from the National Resource Defense Council. But when she took office at the EPA, she was given no guidance by the President who appointed her. He never called a meeting with Ms. Whitman, and he never laid out a specific agenda for her and her agency. Ms. Whitman had only Candidate Bush's speeches as a guide.

In his defense, the President did give Secretary of the Treasury Paul O'Neill the go-ahead to call upon Whitman shortly after they both took office. O'Neill, who had been CEO at Alcoa and

A Letter to America

was unusual because he appears to care about the environment as well as about corporate profits, had developed a global warming paper while he was at Alcoa. Whitman and O'Neill worked on the issue of global warming to create a policy. Appearing before a Congressional committee in early 2001, Whitman told reporters, "There's no question but that global warming is a real phenomenon that is occurring... And while scientists can't predict where droughts will occur, where the flooding will occur precisely, or when, we know those things will occur." This statement seems to be completely in line with Candidate Bush's September 29, 2000, position paper in which he stated that he would push to "establish mandatory reduction targets for emissions of four main pollutants [that contribute to global warming]: sulfur dioxide, nitrogen oxide, mercury and carbon dioxide."

At that point in her tenure, even though she had not yet met personally with the President to discuss the administration's stance on the environment, Ms. Whitman went to Trieste, Italy, to represent the Bush White House and the United States at a G-8 meeting on the environment. But Whitman was flying without a net. Wisely, she called a meeting with Condoleezza Rice, the National Security Advisor, and Andrew Card, the President's Chief of Staff prior to her departure for the meeting. She laid out her environmental plan, which included reduction in the greenhouse gases, that is copper dioxide, sulfur dioxide, nitrogen oxide and mercury. According to Ron Suskind's book *The Price of Loyalty,* "Both Card and Rice told Whitman that the strategy squared with the President's position." So, in Trieste, the EPA Director told the other seven industrial nations that, "The President has said global climate change is the greatest environmental challenge that we face and that we must recognize that and take steps to move forward." Ms. Whitman went on to say that, "the President would oversee bi-partisan legislation to limit carbon dioxide emissions [one of the greenhouse gas most commonly blamed by scientists for trapping heat in the earth's atmosphere], from U.S. power plants for the first time." Whitman followed up her trip with a comprehensive memo about global warming, which she sent to the President. In this memo she outlined the importance of the United States' standing firm on global warming. She also stated that "there was a real fear in the international community that if the US is not willing to discuss the issue within the framework of Kyoto the whole thing [international environmental effort] would fall apart."

Poor Whitman; when you fly without a net, sometimes you fall. Less than a week later, under enormous pressure from a furious coal industry, President Bush reversed our environmental course in a letter to a Republican Senator Chuck Hagel (R-Neb). Suddenly, President Bush decided to abandon policies and/or legislation that might put limitations on carbon dioxide emissions. He made no formal announcement of this change. He held no press conference; he just wrote a letter to Senator Hagel. In that letter the President changed his stance and pledged to reduce global warming through market incentives and other less dramatic and immediately effective techniques. He wrote, "at a time when California has already experienced energy shortages, and other Western states are worried about price and availability of energy this summer, we must be very careful not to take actions that would harm consumers." Additionally, reversing the position Ms. Whitman had announced as his representative, the President said there would be no government mandate to put limits on carbon dioxide emissions. Apparently Bush caved in to lobbyists from the coal industry rather than listening to hundreds of scientists who have more than three decades of data to support the need for these limits. Perhaps President Bush's behavior on this issue shouldn't surprise us, if we recall Texas Senate Bill 766.

This is not the only area of concern about the environment in which President Bush has decided to support industry over the public interest. President Bush has supported higher limits of arsenic in our drinking water. His *Healthy Forest* initiative actually destroys the forest. He has repeatedly attempted to drill for oil and natural gas off the coasts of Florida and Texas and in Alaska. He has even devised a way to recount salmon so that they are no longer on the endangered species list.

During his administration, Bill Clinton had imposed tougher regulations on the amount of arsenic, a compound used in some insecticides and in the bronzing process, which is allowed in the drinking water. He lowered the amount of arsenic to ten parts per billion. It doesn't take an environmentalist or even a physician to understand that a lower the level of arsenic in our drinking water is a good thing for everyone. Surprisingly, though, the Bush administration initially opposed this new, stricter regulation. The state of Nebraska, with the backing of the White House, legally challenged the authority of the EPA to enforce this regulation. Nebraska argued that regulating drinking water was a state responsibility and that the EPA had no jurisdiction. Thankfully for us, the US Court of Appeals upheld the authority of the EPA to enforce the stricter standards.

If the mismanaged arsenic issue is not a good enough indicator of the weakness of President Bush 43's commitment to environmental issues, his *Healthy Forests Restoration Act* completes the picture. This legislation has a very catchy title. If you read the bullet points for this act that are published on the White House's web site, you come away feeling that this is an excellent initiative. This legislation should strengthen public participation in developing forest projects; it should reduce the complexity of environmental analysis using the best data available; and it provides a more effective appeals process that should encourage early public participation in planning projects. All this sounds excellent, but when you read further into the initiative, there is a surprise. It has to do with forest fires. Forest overgrowth was one of the primary causes of the wildfires that ravaged Oregon, California, Arizona, and Nevada during the summer of 2002; and this overgrowth continues to threaten our remaining forests. One of the best parts of the White House initiative is a provision that allows lumber companies voluntarily to thin wooded areas around communities, a procedure that helps to prevent forest fires, or at least to minimize the damage they cause for those who live near them. But the bill allows lumber companies to thin the forest by cutting large diameter trees, the ones that make the lumber companies lots of money. The truth is, large diameter trees are the most fire resistant in the forest. They help reduce the chance of widespread forest fires. So the net effect of this seemingly pro-environment bill is a kick in the face to environmentalists and forests, but a big boost to the logging industry.

According to Vice President Cheney's final report from his National Energy Policy Development Group, the President's energy policy will advance new environmentally-friendly technologies, will develop long-term energy strategies, and will raise the living standards of all Americans. This policy has been severely criticized in the national media because the group met and developed its policy in secret. The process used by Cheney's group appeared to have plenty of input from energy corporations, but almost none from anyone else. Over 400 organizations asked to meet with the Energy group, but only 194 were granted meetings. Of these, 158 were energy companies, twenty-two were labor unions, thirteen were environmental groups, and one was consumer organization. The final energy bill that was recommended by Cheney's committee included $28 billion worth of subsidies and tax breaks for energy corporations. When Vice President Cheney was questioned about what appears to be an energy corporation windfall, he stated that the final plan had eleven of twelve items that the Sierra Club proposed. The Sierra Club shot back, "if Bush really believes these plans are similar [to what we wanted], then Arthur Andersen must be checking his math."

We all know that our nation's energy consumption is enormous. In the year 2002, the United States used approximately 23% of all the energy consumed on earth. The United States makes up approximately 6% of the world's population. To date, our primary energy sources have been oil and natural gas. But clearly these are finite resources. Ever since the late 1970's, it has become clear, given our energy use and our desire to be less dependent upon oil producers in the Middle East, that the United States needs to develop alternative forms of energy, such as solar, wind, hydrogen, and nuclear power. But it appears that President Bush 43 thinks it is more important for us to increase exploration for and drilling of oil and natural gas. To this end, he has supported, or at least not stood in the way of, the energy companies' initiatives mentioned above, thus leaving our National Parks, our coast lines, and the Alaskan wildlife refuge in jeopardy. In his 2003 State of the Union address, President Bush told us, "Tonight I'm proposing $1.2 billion in research funding so that America can lead the world in developing clean, hydrogen-powered automobiles." $1.2 billion sounds like a lot of money, but when the total budget for the federal government is over $2.4 trillion, it is easy to do the numbers and see that Bush is asking for only a very small part of our budget (less than 0.01%) for one of our very biggest national problems. For comparison purposes, consider this: Ford, DaimlerChrysler, BMW, GM, Honda, and Toyota have all developed hydrogen cars that work. DaimlerChrysler alone spends over $5 billion a year in research and development. In this light, our

President's proposal reveals a lack of true commitment to hydrogen technology.

Equally disturbing on the environmental front is this administration's support of various energy companies' initiatives to begin natural gas and oil drilling in or near some of our most beautiful and fragile natural areas. These companies have fought to drill for natural gas in our National Parks. They have fought to drill for oil off the Texas coast, near the popular vacation spot of Padre Island, and off the coast of Florida, near Destin, which is one of America's most beautiful Gulf Coast beaches. They have tried on two occasions to drill in the Arctic National Wildlife Refuge in Alaska. Bush 43's response to these activities is troubling. Instead of taking a firm stand to resist these industries' eagerness to exploit some of our last and most beautiful natural areas, he appears to be waffling; or, even worse, he has begun to support increased exploration and drilling.

Yet another example of President Bush's strange way of supporting environmental issues can be seen in how he has recently responded to the question under debate about whether or not we should protect salmon as an endangered species. In order to determine whether salmon should be classified as an endangered species, it is necessary to count salmon. Just what size is the population of this species today? In a classical move, which supports industry over the environment, the Bush administration decided to count salmon hatched in fisheries along with those born in the wild. Obviously, this will inflate the numbers, and make it less likely that environmental groups could make the argument that salmon are endangered.

One last example of President Bush's failure to protect our environment involves his administration's response to the need to reauthorize taxes to support the 1980 Superfund Act, which was established to help clean up the environment. The Superfund has allowed cleanup of some of our worst environmental disasters using a combination of money from the government and from the guilty polluters. The Superfund was started in respond to New York's Love Canal and Kentucky's Valley of Drums. Upon its passing, the act levied a tax on corporations to help pay for the fund. This is poetic justice, for much of the clean up was aimed at areas that big business had dirtied. When President Bush took office in 2001, the fund had approximately $860 million; not a huge sum, but certainly helpful in dealing with environmental problems. Currently the fund has less than $28 million, but according to a recent report from CNN, the Bush administration has no intention of asking Congress to reauthorize corporate taxes to build this fund back up.

Almost monthly, President boards Air Force One and uses jet fuel to fly to his country —retreat, his ranch in Crawford, Texas. There, he rides horses in the open air, he fishes in some of that property's many lakes, clearly enjoying a clean and healthy environment. Ironically, while he enjoys the rewards of having open space and clean air himself, this President is slowly dismantling thirty years of environmental legislation that is meant to make sure that you and I can enjoy similar pleasures.

Chapter 10 – Leadership – There is a Difference between Wandering and Leading

Over 2500 years ago Sun Tzu wrote *The Art of War*, possibly the definitive work on conflict. This ancient work has much to say about leadership. In the opening chapter Sun Tzu states that leadership is a matter of five ancient and seemingly universal characteristics.

The best example of George Bush's leadership should come from his greatest challenge— September 11, 2001. On that day, President Bush had an opportunity to show the nation his ability to lead. Where was our President on September 11, 2001? What was he doing? What decisions did he make? How did he lead the nation during that time of shocking and seemingly unprovoked crisis?

The President started the day at the Emma E. Booker Elementary School in Sarasota, Florida, around 9:00 A.M. He was scheduled to read to the schoolchildren. Exactly when he was informed that the first plane crashed into the World Trade Center is unclear. The President and his staff have given several conflicting reports. The President stated, "First of all, when we walked into the classroom, I had seen this plane fly into the first building. There was a TV set on. And you know, I thought it was pilot error, and I was amazed that anybody could make such a terrible mistake." It is clear that the President's motorcade did not leave the elementary school until 9:35 A.M., which was more than fifty minutes after CNN broadcast the first airplane's crashing into the World Trade Center.

By 9:35 A.M., Richard Clarke, the White House Counter Terrorism Advisor, had briefly met with the National Security Advisor Condoleezza Rice and Vice President Cheney at the White House. Clarke had given the order to evacuate the White House of all nonessential personnel, and then went to the Secure Video Conferencing Center in the White House. In this room, Richard Clarke could communicate with the Defense Department, the CIA, the State Department, the Joint Chiefs of Staff, and other essential government organizations, including the FAA. It was Richard Clarke, not our President, who decided to ask Jane Garvey, the administrator of the FAA, because the Secretary of Transportation, Norman Mineta, Jane Garvey's boss, could not be found early in the crisis, to take the extraordinary step of grounding all aircraft flying in American air space. Clarke also coordinated Combat Air Patrol over Washington DC and New York, placing fighter jets in the air over these cities. It was now 9:28 A.M. The President was still in an elementary school

A Letter to America

in Florida. Richard Clarke continued to coordinate our response to the crisis. He suggested closing all of our overseas embassies to Richard Armitage, Deputy Secretary of State. Clarke and Armitage decided to call the Soviets and inform them of the crisis, since the country and the Department of Defense had gone into war mode. The Russian were on the verge of starting an exercise with all of their strategic nuclear forces. Without that call from Armitage, one could imagine a scenario in which things could have gotten farther out of control than they already were. Brian Stafford, Director of the Secret Service, was also in the Secure Video Conferencing Center. He requested fighter escorts for Air Force One. It was Clarke who asked to secure authority from the President (thru the Vice President) for the Air Force to "shoot down any aircraft – including a hijacked passenger flight – that looks like it is threatening to attack and cause large-scale death on the ground." Amazingly, the President of the United States appeared to be completely uninvolved in the 9/11 crisis until this point. He had been informed and had been on the phone to Cheney, but I can find no accounts of any orders that the President gave until he boarded Air Force One at 9:55 A.M., an hour and nine minutes after the attacks began.

At 9:30 A.M. President Bush did take the initiative to address the nation from the Booker Elementary School. "Today we had a national tragedy. Two planes have crashed into the World Trade Center in an apparent terrorist attack upon our country." His address told us what had happened, that we were at risk, but it did little to relieve our anxiety or demonstrate leadership.

Early in this crisis there was uncertainty everywhere. It was unclear how many targets there were or where those targets might be. Was the President himself a target? Mr. Bush's own father had been a target of Muslim extremists. Nevertheless, when Air Force One took off from the runway in Sarasota, Florida, at 9:55 A.M., it was without a fighter escort. Why? And, for that matter, where was Air Force One going? Was the President safer in the air than on the ground, even though several flying aircraft were thought to be hijacked? Several reporters on Air Force One thought that the President's plane was flying in circles, since the Sarasota TV stations continued to get good reception. Where might we expect our President to head at that time? To Washington? To New York? To the safe bunker? Instead, we were told that he flew to Barksdale Air Force Base in Louisiana. How odd. What were he and his advisors and protectors thinking?

Hundreds of command decisions were made in the first hours after American Airlines Flight 11 crashed into the North tower of the World Trade Center. Some of the decisions, already mentioned, were unprecedented. The FAA grounded all air travel in the United States. The White House was evacuated. All government buildings in Washington and all national landmarks as well as Disney World and the Sears Tower were evacuated. Combat air patrol began over all major cities. Aircraft carriers and battleships steamed towards New York to secure the harbor. The Coast Guard closed all harbors to any traffic but that of our Navy. The Continuity of Government Program, an administrative operation that had been in place since

A Letter to America

the Cold War, which takes key leaders to secure locations, was also activated. Yet almost all of these decisions were not made by the President himself, they were either the result of well-established protocols or made by lesser officials. While one might argue that it is good that our government has contingency plans that seem to work in a crisis, it is still true that our President only made one decision during the first critical hour. How can we know if during that time he displayed any of Sun Tzu's list of the attributes of a great leader: intelligence, trustworthiness, humaneness, courage, and sternness?

Turning attention away from the crisis of 9/11, which has given us a sketchy, and perhaps carefully managed or "spun" idea of the President's leadership skills, consider President Bush's leadership during the corporate scandals which began to break into our national consciousness in 2002. The first corporation to go bad was Enron. In early 2002 it was clear that Enron had developed an elaborate scheme to hide debt. In addition to Enron, WorldCom, Adelphia, Arthur Andersen, and Tyco were also under investigation for corporate malfeasance. Investors had lost billions of dollars. Tens of thousands of workers had been laid off. The country was looking toward Washington, and especially toward the White House, for guidance and leadership. For certainly it was not unreasonable for us to expect the government to take steps to prevent this type of criminal behavior on the parts of our captains of industry, not to mention the horrible consequences their actions brought about for so many everyday American citizens.

During the early days of these corporate scandals, on June 28, 2002, Mr. Bush told the nation "it's important for our fellow citizens to understand that, by far, the vast majority of our leaders in the business community are honest and upright people." Sadly, this statement was contradicted by a *Business Week* poll, which revealed that 55% of CFOs had been asked by corporate executives to misrepresent the corporation's true performance and 12% admitted that they had lied about their corporate earnings.

As the situation in our vast business community began to get worse, or, more likely, as the realities of what had been going on for years began to be made public, President Bush, finally addressed a meeting of several hundred CEO's on July 9, 2002. It was in this speech that George W. Bush might have shown some leadership, despite the fact that he had many friends and financial backers in the corporate world. (For example, Kenneth Lay, Enron's CEO, had been a huge contributor —over $750,000 personally donated— to George W. Bush in both his presidential campaign and his gubernatorial campaign as well as to the Republican Party.) The President told his audience and the nation, "And so again today I'm calling for a new ethic of personal responsibility in the business community; an ethic that will increase investor confidence, will make employees proud of their companies, and again, regain the trust of the American people." He went on to say, "First, we will use the full weight of the law to expose and root out corruption. My administration will do everything in our power to end the days of cooking the books, shading the truth, and breaking our laws." He then the President pledged $100 million

A Letter to America

in additional funding to help clean up corporate corruption. (Because of budget cuts by the Bush White House in 2002, the SEC had to lay off over 50 workers. This is in direct contrast to the 60% increase in the number of complaints from 2001 to 2002 making $100 million increase woefully inadequate.)

President Bush really said nothing of significant substance for the rest of his speech. The speech was littered with phrases such as, "The vast majority of businessmen and women are honest," and "we need men and women of character, who know the difference between ambition and destructive greed," and "our schools of business must be principled teachers of right and wrong, and [should] not surrender to moral confusion and relativism ." These are hollow and empty statements. He has not supported any of the specific legislation that corporate reformers have been asking for, such as those cited in an article in *Time Magazine* on June 17, 2002. The corporate reformers urged the following: that corporate board members must be held accountable for their corporate reports, that the CEO of a company cannot serve as its Chairman of the Board, that consulting firms should not also act as auditors of the same company, that the rocketing salaries of CEOs ought to be limited, that CEOs should not be allowed to sell stock twelve months prior to a corporate bankruptcy, that stock options should be counted as a company expense, and finally that companies should stop the practice of giving loans to executives. All these proposals, if properly enforced, would help to decrease corporate craziness and increase investor confidence. To date, the President has not shown any evidence that he is ready to lead the country into reforms such as these.

Interestingly, President Bush did choose to support the last reform in this list. He told the nation, "... I challenge compensation committees to put an end to all company loans to corporate officers." This could quite possibly have been Mr. Bush's most hypocritical statement of his presidency. In 1986, when Mr. Bush was not yet even a governor, he was on the board of Harken Energy Corporation. This is a small oil company in Texas. Mr. Bush received a low interest loan, below the prime rate, for $96,000, from Harken, which he used to buy 80,000 shares of stock in the company. Later, in 1988, he was again loaned over $84,000 by Harken to buy 25,000 more shares of Harken stock. Every day folks, including the employees at Harken who could use just such a loan, can only dream of such sweet deals coming their way. If this weren't bad enough, Bush held the stock for several years and then sold it on June 22, 1990. Two months later, the company announced huge losses, which caused the stock value to plummet. As chairman of the Harken board's audit committee, Bush must have had some inkling about what was going to happen to the company and, therefore, to the value of his own shares. These actions are far more egregious, I would suggest, than the ones that have recently caused Martha Stewart to be sentenced to jail time. But let us look at the larger issue: Did anything Mr. Bush say or propose anything to help reform corporate greed? Were any of his empty statements going to make a difference in our corporate problems? Wall Street didn't think so. The Dow dropped 282 points following his speech on corporate responsibility. So how is our President doing as an economic leader? Sun Tzu would have an answer, one that I believe isn't likely to help Mr. Bush get re-elected in November.

When I think about what has happened in our country and the world over the past four years, my mind races with ideas. Some might be crazy, but others, I think are—or *were*—within the realm of possibility. Let me play out some of my fantasies for you. The American President, immediately after 9/11, instead of alienating the world as he has with the Iraq fiasco, would find ways to put all the world's goodwill, energy, and resources together to combat global terrorism. He would see to it that governments share intelligence fully and honestly.

In Afghanistan, he would have formed an international coalition and sent enough trained troops to deal with the Taliban and Osama Bin Laden appropriately from the start. He would not have waited more than sixty days before sending a large force. The invasion would not have consisted of conventional forces, but, instead, of groups of highly trained Special Forces. These Special Forces would have broken up into small teams and surgically excised terrorists where ever their fresh new intelligence told them they were. This brings me to another fantasy: that our intelligence would be first rate, that our own agents would speak the languages of our enemies, and that all intelligence gathering communities would be in better communication. There would have been little or no collateral damage. Villages and wedding parties would not have been mistakenly bombed. The number of innocents killed would not have been in the thousands. We would have accomplished our goal of capturing or destroying the Taliban. We would have captured Osama bin Laden cowering in the caves of the Tora Bora Mountains. In my fantasy, the international community would also have taken on some of the expense of the Afghanistan war and of reconstructing that nation.

With the capture of high-ranking officials in both al Qaeda and the Taliban, this international coalition could then turn its attention to other countries that harbor or support terrorism. Armed with their successes the moral superiority they had earned by being a multinational force, this coalition could effectively pressure Saudi Arabia, the home of the majority of the 9-11 terrorists, into better cooperation. Funding for terrorism in Saudi Arabia would be squelched. The preaching of hate by Islamic extremists would be condemned. At the same time, Iran would be pressured by the Muslim world and the international community not only to stop sponsoring terrorism, but also to stop their nuclear weapons program. If diplomatic persuasion did not work, the coalition would have international support to again swing into action and force a rogue nation to comply with universal standards of decency, humanity, and freedom.

In my fantasy, if the international community spoke with one loud and clear voice, North Korea might be brought back to the negotiating table. If the international community presented financial incentives, such as food and energy, it might persuade the North Koreans to stop building nuclear weapons and to dismantle its existing weapons of mass destruction.

Can you imagine a leader with such vision? Only an intelligent, trustworthy, humane, courageous, and stern leader could have pulled off such magic. America needed such a leader on September 12, 2001, and it needs such a leader today. Unfortunately, President Bush 43 does not measure up to Sun Tzu's yardstick. I truly wish he did.

My friends, I thank you for reading my letter. I have tried to explain the issues to the best of my ability, if I have not always gotten it right, you are smart folks, correct me, and help us look more clearly and with better information at what has become of this nation we love so much and that teeters, I fear on the brink of unimaginable disaster. Inform yourselves, this isn't rocket science or brain surgery I've been writing to you about—join the national debate; dream with me of a better America, and help us make our dreams come true. God Bless.

Sincerely,

Errington

Errington C. Thompson, MD

About the Author

Errington C. Thompson, MD, surgeon, scholar, fulltime sports fan and part-time political activist. He is active in a number of community projects and initiatives. Through medicine, he strives to improve the physical health of all he treats. Through this book, he hopes to share his thoughts and reflections on the current political landscape. Dr. Thompson, educated at Emory University and Southwestern Medical School, currently resides in Northeast Texas.

Printed in the United States
26356LVS00004B/181-183